THE MAYA CIVILIZATION

BY

GEORGE W. BRAINERD

LOS ANGELES

SOUTHWEST MUSEUM

1954

REPRINTED 1963

Lithographed in U.S.A. by

E D W A R D S   B R O T H E R S ,   I N C .

Ann Arbor, Michigan

CONTENTS

ILLUSTRATIONS

I—INTRODUCTION

THE Maya civilization, unlike that of the Aztecs and Incas, did not excite the wonder and the cupidity of the first Europeans who wandered over the New World. For at 1500 A. D. the Maya people were harried and disunited, their magnificent religious centers deserted, the power of their haughty priests broken. They lived in a world of uncertainty in fear of more militaristic neighbors, anchored by their farming, their traditions, their pilgrimages to ancient shrines. And the descendants of the ancient Maya still live in their native country, a withdrawn, self-contained people, their outlook on the world mellowed but subdued by observation of peoples more active, but perhaps less wise; the Toltecs and Aztecs, the Spanish, the modern Mexicans with their enthusiasm for ancient times, the amazing but barbarous Yanquis. Their Catholicism has settled upon them like a garment, molded to the firm underlying form of the ancient, agriculturally-based Maya religion. European civilization has given them the steel machete, pigs and chickens, but little else which they would not gladly spare.

These people, now quiet, friendly, fatalistic, were the intellectuals of the New World. Their writing system, calendar, arts, and architecture were the finest of the Americas. The unique cultural attainments of the Maya and the peculiar character of the Maya settlement plan and economy were developed in a densely vegetated lowland tropical area, an unusal environment for a high culture, and one which should be examined for an understanding of these people.

ENVIRONMENT

The Maya country is varied in its climate and physiography. The center of greatest development was in the lowlands of northern Guatemala and adjacent Mexico, but also included the Guatemala highlands, the Yucatan Peninsula, the area stretching northwest to the Isthmus of Tehuantepec, and southwest into Honduras and El Salvador. On the east

*A general text of this sort always depends for the major part of its information on the work of people other than the author. This is particularly true for Maya archeology, a study so specialized that no single individual can qualify fully as an expert on all of its aspects. I am particularly indebted to A. M. Tozzer, A. V. Kidder, and Tatiana Proskouriakoff for critical reading of my text and to the staff of the Carnegie Institution of Washington, Department of Archeology, for my introduction to the field. Many interpretations of the data are my own responsibility. Illustrations not made by the author are acknowledged in their captions.

Mexican coast in northern Vera Cruz the Huastec Indians
speak a Maya tongue, and must once have been the northern
outlyers of culturally-related groups of Maya-speaking people
who lined the southern half of the shoreline of the Gulf of
Mexico (map 1). Nearly all of this area lies in the northern
tropical belt. Its climate is characterized by a pronounced
rainy season in summer and fall, and little rain during the rest
of the year. Temperature is mild, allowing light housing save
in the mountainous Guatemala highlands, but even here
freezing weather rarely occurs.

The northern Guatemalan lowland area of the Peten,
where the Maya ritualistic developments attained their greatest
height, is densely covered with 'high bush', tropical forest
with tall trees along the ridge-like hills which run roughly
east and west through the area. These hills alternate with
depressed areas which, usually lacking a regular drainage
pattern, turn to swamps or temporary lakes during the
rainy season, and bear either stands of high grass, the savannas,
or support dense thickets of water-loving plants and trees.
Limestone underlies this area, and there is considerable underground drainage. The ground-water usually lies too deep for
primitive human use, although there are a few lakes and a
number of waterholes, some of which last through most dry
seasons. This area is at present almost completely unpopulated, and is one of the most difficult areas in the Americas
for both modern agriculture and transportation. Its heavy
cosmopolitan population in ancient times gives striking testi-
mony of the gulf between the Maya ways of livelihood and
ours.

To the south of the above described lowland area in the
Guatemalan Department of the Peten rise the Guatemalan
highlands cut by the Motagua River drainage. These are more
rugged areas with a cooler climate, better drainage, and more
evenly distributed rainfall. The lack of elaborate architecture
here may be laid to the absence of limestone and the frequent
earthquakes.

In traveling north from the central Maya area the limestone ridges become lower and less regular in placement, the
climate dryer, the bush grows, at least under the present agricultural customs, to a height of about thirty feet. Rainfall
grows progressively lighter to the northwest, stunting and
changing the types of plants which throughout most of
Yucatan include many desert species. Soil in Yucatan seldom
exceeds six inches to a foot deep, and thus cannot be plowed. It
consists for the greater part of a leached-out red clay which fills

the fissures in the underlying limestone. This relatively dry country is made inhabitable through the year by the presence of the famous cenotes, deep caves or open pits in the limestone, which often hold permanent water in their bottoms. Yucatan is the most populous part of the Maya area at the present time (about 30 persons per square mile). Nearly all of the area is under use. Henequen- and cattle-raising are important in dryer areas; corn is raised over almost the whole territory and is the staple food. In the few areas of Yucatan with deeper soil, sugar-cane is produced. Although modern Yucatan has the qualities of an island, with negligible overland communication, it is unsafe to assume that this was true in times before roads and railroads were essentials for transportation. This modern insularity of Yucatan has made her look more to the United States and to Cuba, and less to the Mexican mainland, than do other Mexican regions. The modern Yucatecans consider Mexico somewhat of a foreign country; their Maya forebears certainly did the same.

PHYSICAL CHARACTERISTICS

The Maya people still form a majority of the population of the Maya area. This situation exists in but few regions of the United States, where European settlers have usually driven the earlier inhabitants to extinction or to an impoverished existence on poor land. The distribution of Maya family names in Yucatan still conforms to the ancient Maya political divisions; the people have clung to their lands as well as to their traditions.

The physique of the Maya seems more constant among individuals than is that of most groups of men, and this may be the result of much contact among them in the past, combined with but slight interbreeding with other groups. They are rather short, long-bodied, light-boned but chunky, with good muscle development and a tendency toward an overlay of fat. Heads are broad, lips delicately modeled and rather prominent, noses have a high convex bridge and curved pendulous tip, chin and forehead are

FIG. 1—A MAYA FARMER
(T. A. Willard photo.)

somewhat receding, eyes have a Mongoloid cast with heavy lids, and cheekbones are prominent. Skin-color varies from medium to dark-brown, hair is black, straight to rarely wavy, graying relatively late in life, there is some tendency toward baldness in older women. Their resemblance to the people pictured in the art of the Maya cultural heyday is striking.

The emotional stability and cultural conservatism which characterize the Yucatecan Maya has been mentioned above; among the highland Maya these qualities seem less pronounced, but modern psychological attitudes as well as cultural habits are learned and changeable, and are but an uncertain evidence of these qualities in the past. A greater physical variability among the Highland Maya, the linguistic diversity, and the historical accounts all suggest that they have been subject to much more outside influence than have the lowland peoples.

The modern Yucatan Maya value personal cleanliness very highly and bathe once or oftener daily. Their thatch houses are scantily furnished and almost always neat. Numerous vestiges of pre-Conquest religious customs are still observable in the country, particularly those connected with corn agriculture and, to a lesser degree, with other aspects of personal and family life.

The Maya language is spoken by most Yucatecans, many of whom do not speak Spanish. There is some evidence of impoverishment of Maya vocabulary over the last 200 years, but the language is still in good form, and many Maya place-names are in common and widespread use even for the main towns which have borne their Spanish-given names for 400 years. Many of the Yucatan Maya also cherish the traditions of their descent which are carried down in families, and they make pilgrimages to ancient Maya ruins, in some cases to offer sacrifices. The later occupied of the Maya ruins, in several instances, have retained locally what must have been their original names, whereas older ruins have been given names descriptive of their modern appearance.

Although we have sound archeological evidence of the military occupancy of Yucatan by Mexican mainland peoples 500 or 600 years before the Conquest, and of close relations between the Aztecs and Yucatan from then until the time of the Spanish Conquest, surprisingly little linguistic or cultural evidence of this has survived. The Maya cultural roots must have been strong; a thousand years of constant repression has not eradicated them! The vestiges of the Maya culture which have best incorporated themselves into the modern Yucatan folk-culture are, as would be expected, those

FIG. 2.—MAYA THATCH-ROOFED VILLAGE HOUSE

connected with the everyday life of the common man. These traits are the hardest kind of thing to get at archeologically in this area, and thus are particularly well adapted to supplement the findings of archeology, the most accessible of which pertain to the elaborately organized politico-religious system which once unified the Maya.

The history of the Maya must be approached indirectly; we have no authoritative written records of their past. But this is true of most of man's history everywhere. The first words were written less than five thousand years ago, only a two-hundredth part of the million years man has lived on the world, and we have no decipherable written records of New World history. We are dependent on archeology for our knowledge of the Maya, and our archeological record in the Maya area at present goes back to only a thousand years or so before Christ. Archeological history is apt to be a one-sided story, with none of the wealth of incident which gives written history its sparkle. But we can tell the story of technical and intellectual achievements, and from the buildings and arts of the people can hope to absorb some of the flavor of this remarkable culture.

There are several general texts which treat of the Maya. Those most useful for the beginner are:

Morley, S. G., *The Ancient Maya*, Stanford, 1946. Spinden, H. S., *Ancient Civilization of Mexico and Central America*, New York, 1922. *The Maya and Their Neighbors*, New York, 1940. All of these contain bibliographies which will aid the reader to go further into specialized fields that may interest him, as well as a list of titles on Maya geography and physical anthropology. Vaillant, G. C., *The Aztecs of Mexico*, New York, 1941 (also republished as a Pelican book), gives a lively account of a civilization which paralleled the Maya to some degree, and thus makes good supplementary reading.

II—THE FORMATIVE STAGE

Our earliest knowledge of the people of the Maya area comes from excavations at Uaxactun in the Department of the Peten, Guatemala; from the ruins of Kaminaljuyu near Guatemala City in the highlands; from the Guatemala West Coast; from Tres Zapotes in southern Vera Cruz; from various locations in Honduras, British Honduras, Yucatan, and Campeche; and from as far north as Tampico, Vera Cruz (map 1). Excavations at all these points show people who were pottery-using agriculturists who seem not yet to have evolved the elaborate and extensive religious centers characteristic of the later Classic stage Maya. These points, with their wide geographic range, represent simply locations which happen to have been excavated archeologically; certainly the whole Maya area may be assumed to have been occupied by similar people. The remains found have been classified, for convenience of description, into the Pre-Classic or Formative stage of development of the Maya culture, and this stage may be defined by the characteristics of culture which its archeological sites show in common. Although there is considerable similarity among remains from these sites as compared to others in meso America, and the area which includes them corresponds in general to that in which the Maya tongues are spoken, there is, of course, no proof that all of this area, and only this, was "Maya" in early times and indeed only a part of it later developed a Classic Maya culture. The date of Formative beginnings may be estimated, on information from other areas, at 1500 or 2000 B.C. The Formative stage ended with the beginning of Maya hieroglyphically inscribed stone monuments, believed to be at about 300 A.D.

There is evidence that by 2000 B.C. or somewhat earlier, the whole meso American region, which extends from an east-west line somewhat north of Mexico City to part-way through El Salvador and Honduras, was inhabited by horticultural peoples who probably depended on corn for their main carbohydrate food, although conceivably manioc may have been important in part or all of the lowland areas, and for proteins and minerals they depended on beans, wild game and fish, fruits and a variety of vegetal products. We know that in the Valley of Mexico during these times the people lived in villages, used cotton cloth, and worshiped deities who likely were connected with agriculture. Although no settlement of this date within the Maya area has been thoroughly excavated, the evidence available suggests that there was already much similarity and intercommunication throughout meso America during this time.

ARCHEOLOGICAL CHARACTERISTICS

The archeological characteristics which allow the Maya Formative sites to be related to one another in time can be defined most fully in their pottery. In fact, pottery is by all odds the most sensitive diagnostic for the chronological placement of Maya archeological deposits. Formative pottery is nearly exclusively monochrome. The finer vessels are covered by a slip or coating of colored clay, brushed onto the smooth surface of the unfired vessel, and often burnished with a tool before firing. Vessel forms are simple, legs are commonly found only on vessels of the later part of the stage. Decoration in the form of grooving and incision is common. From the Guatemala highlands and mainland Mexico come figurines, some with movable arms and legs, and both cylindrical and flat pottery stamps with carved designs.

It is in the Guatemala highlands that the most elaborate Formative ceramics of the Maya area have been found; these are comparable in development to the recent finds from the Formative cemetery of Tlatilco in the Valley of Mexico (outside the Maya area). While this fact suggests that the high-

FIG. 3—FORMATIVE POTTERY FROM THE GUATEMALA HIGHLANDS (after Shook). *a-e*, *h*, bear red paint on light-colored slips. *f* bears a negative painted design, *g* is gray-brown in color. *a* and *b* are incised; *g* is grooved; *c* bears an appliqued head; the legs of *f* are hollow, bearing pellets.

land country was a center to which the lowland areas were provincial during these times, it is also possible that this appearance of advancement is due to the fact that the elaborate archeological remains of this area come from tombs of notables. From these rich tombs is derived evidence for good lapidary work in hard stone, painting on a gesso coating over pottery, and, most surprisingly, evidence for the stirrup pot and the whistling jar, two elaborate pottery forms best known through numerous later examples from Peruvian graves.

Toward the later end of the Formative stage several ceramic innovations are recognizable. A second color, painted in bands or in simple, broadly drawn, usually abstract designs over the slip color, became common. This dichrome painting is often outlined by an incised line, and areas of the design are sometimes stippled with depressions made in the clay. In later

Formative or early Classic times, the incision was replaced by black or white outlining to produce the earliest of the polychrome painted pottery which reached such heights during the Classic stage which followed. A new technique of drawing with a paint which often produced reverse or negative designs on the slip was also very popular in late Formative times. Vessel-legs became commoner and increased in size, many of them being hollow and provided with pellets to serve as rattles. The composite or keeled bowl, distinguished by an angular break in wall contour, also is characteristic of the late Formative stage; a narrow-mouthed jar with a teapot-like spout is widespread, and at the end of the stage often was made with a bridge linking the spout to the jar-neck.

Work in stone was well advanced. Obsidian blades of superlative technique, well-ground axes and chisels, fine jade carvings, stone effigies of mushroom form are found. A full-sized ceremonial mask composed of finely carved and polished green-stone elements was recovered from a Kaminaljuyu tomb. There is also evidence that stone monuments bearing low-relief sculpture were first made in Formative times, although Maya-style datable stelae are a hallmark of the Classic stage.

SOCIAL ORGANIZATION

These archeological criteria allow the identification of the remains of the Formative stage in the Maya area, but do not, without some interpretation, tell much of the people who made them. Most of the material described thus far has come from soundings or trenches; careful excavations of large areas, which might allow the identification of houses and settlement plans, and of a more complete range of domestic utensils, have not been made in any number. Kidder has suggested, from surface archeological survey, that at Kaminaljuyu the Formative settlement may have been a large town in contrast to the overlying Classic remains at the same site which appear to represent only a religious center or cemetery. Evidence of mud-daubed wattlework house-walls has also come to light; and a multitude of refuse-filled bottle-shape pits, the use of which is still uncertain. Vaillant believed that the Middle Culture remains in the Valley of Mexico, which belong within this time-span, were of villages. It is well possible that all or a major part of the Formative settlements of the Maya area may have been towns or villages, but the absence of evidence for such settlements during the Classic stage makes their earlier presence an assumption which cannot be safely made without more excavation. The kind of house used was very likely not far different from the dwellings of today: simple thatch-roofed structures with either mud-laid stone or wattlework walls, a cool and efficient type in the mild climate of the area. This house-type is shown in Maya Classic stage sculpture and exhibits considerable homogeneity over the Maya area at present. The food of the people was probably largely corn, as it still is, supplemented with beans, fruits, and what meat and fish could be caught.

Of the religion of the early Formative Maya, we know little, but can suspect a considerable elaboration from the evidence of its high development and formality toward the end of Formative times. Simple hand-modeled clay figurines come from certain of the Maya early Formative sites, and may well have been used for private religious worship. There is internal evidence from Maya calendrics which suggests that continual astronomical observations were kept during late Formative times which suggests that the highly organized group of priests, who dominated the Maya during the Classic stage, may have commenced their singularly conservative but enlightened sway this early.

The earliest evidence of the evolution of complex societies in both the Old and New Worlds is based on the finding of elaborate public works. Large structures indicate the degree of social organization required to rear them. Manpower must be organized and directed; to do so requires a government. The structure must be planned, and if its decoration is elaborate, skilled artizans must be available. The exact date of the first large Maya structures is unknown; we likewise do not know in which part of the Maya area they appear earliest. In the state of Campeche, Mexico, at Santa Rosa Xtampak, an excavation under a Classic Maya plaza floor showed ten feet or more of stone fill dated by pottery to the Middle Formative substage. There is reason to believe that this mass of stone is part of a substructure on which an altar or temple had been built. At Yaxuna, Yucatan, a large substructure of Late Formative date is known which seems to have been surmounted by several buildings. At Uaxactun, Guatemala, stands a small square, stucco-covered, stepped pyramid (fig. 4) on which a thatch-roofed temple probably once stood. This substructure bears four staircases flanked by huge, elaborately modeled stucco faces in a highly conventionalized style obviously related to that of Classic Maya religious art. It was built either in late Formative or very early Classic times. At Kaminaljuyu, in the Guatemala highlands, a large late Formative temple-bearing pyramid has recently been excavated and found to overlie a series of elaborate tombs, and a sizable pyramid of the earliest Formative period containing a cache of elaborate artifacts has been found.

These early structures are in the form of step-sided pyramids, and were used as the foundations of altars and temples. Their height must have added materially to the impressiveness of the ceremonies performed on top of them which were viewed by thousands of worshippers from the large floored plazas below. This use of pyramids is in general quite different from that of the Egyptians, but somewhat similar to the use of the

FIG. 4—A FORMATIVE OR EARLY CLASSIC STAGE MAYA SUBSTRUCTURE, E-VII SUB AT UAXACTUN, GUATEMALA. (AFTER PROSKOURIAKOFF)

Mesopotamian ziggurats, although the meso American pyramids were certainly independently invented; we know of no intercommunication between the Old World and the New during this and the following time periods. There is evidence that the large substructures in the Guatemala highlands were built to contain the richly furnished tombs of local notables, after which temples were erected on their summits; this custom seems to represent a regional variation from the general use of pyramidal structures in meso America and seems to have lasted in some areas from late Formative times until the European conquest. A somewhat similar custom of burial in pyramidal mounds was followed in early times in the Mississippi

Valley where it was later replaced by the use of pyramids solely as temple substructures.

Estimates of the amount and kinds of labor required to raise these large substructures may give some clue as to the size and social organization of the groups who built them. The pyramids of the Sun and Moon at Teotihuacan in the Valley of Mexico are probably Formative, and are the largest of the meso American structures. The Pyramid of the Sun covers nearly the same area as the largest of the Egyptian pyramids, although, due to its lower height, it has only about one quarter of the volume—about 1,000,000 cubic meters. The Pyramid of the Moon at Teotihuacan, which dates from about the same time, contains more than 250,000 cubic meters of fill. The amount of both skilled and unskilled labor required to raise the Pyramid of the Sun was far lower in comparison with the Egyptian pyramids than these figures indicate, since the Pyramid of Cheops is built of tightly fitted, carefully cut stone blocks of tremendous size, while the Teotihuacan substructures are merely stone and stucco faced over a simple earth fill. The Cuicuilco mound, also in the Valley of Mexico, and probably of earlier date, contains about 100,000 cubic meters of earth; it is faced with boulders, rather than with quarried stone as used at Teotihuacan. At Kaminaljuyu, on the outskirts of Guatemala City, is a flat-topped, rectangular pyramid about 20 meters high, which must have approximated the volume of the Cuicuilco mound. It is made chiefly of adobe, without a stone facing. It is quite likely that each of these large substructures grew as the result of several additions.

It is reasonable to assume that the cores of meso American pyramids were erected by the unskilled manpower of the community which was available in the spare time left by their predominately agricultural pursuits. Some idea of the available manpower may be gained if we allow an arbitrary estimate of 100 days of communal labor per year for each man, and compute labor from volume of pyramid fill. This estimate of working time, and the other estimates which follow, are all believed to be maximum; performance very likely was not nearly as high as the estimates given. A man can carry perhaps 1500 pounds of earth or stone per day to the pyramid. This weight will fill a space of 10 cubic feet; thus 3,000,000 man-days of labor would be required for the Pyramid of the Sun, and about 300,000 man-days each for the Cuicuilco and Kaminaljuyu pyramids. Using the figure above, the man-years would run over 30,000 and 3,000 respectively for the cores of these large pyramids. The core of the

Pyramid of the Sun could thus be amassed by 1500 men working over a 20 year period. The number of skilled artisans needed to cut, finish, and build the pyramid casing, direct the labor and aid in the accurate placement of earth, is more difficult to estimate, and would certainly have depended on the type of finish used, source of materials and other factors. Perhaps an estimate of one-fifth the labor force over the same time-period is reasonable. Thus for the erection of the Pyramid of the Sun a minimal force over a twenty-year period (a very arbitrary choice of time) would be 1800 men, which suggests a minimal population of nearly 10,000 people contributing. The actual number of people may have been two, three, or more times this, due to low efficiency of work and if other smaller projects were under way simultaneously a correspondingly larger number of people must have been concerned.

A single Formative village could not have furnished such a labor force, and we are thus forced to the conclusion that groups drawn from a larger area of country, perhaps including several villages, or alternately, a single, very large community or "city" must have been concerned, and thus have been under some sort of a political government, likely ruled by the priests of the local religion. The huge size of the early Classic stage site of Teotihuacan, suggests that community size may have been increasing rapidly through late Formative times in the Valley of Mexico.

The Formative substructures from the Maya lowland area, and for that matter the later Classic Maya substructures, do not approach the Temple of the Sun in size. E VII Sub at Uaxactun has a volume of less than 200 cubic meters. The large late Formative pyramid at Yaxuna is estimated at 50,000 cubic meters, only half the volume of the Cuicuilco pyramid, but large in comparison to most Maya substructures. Maya substructures are characteristically ornate, are topped by elaborate temples and faced with mortared masonry. From Morris' estimates we may compute that one-sixteenth of the volume of a lowland Maya structure is lime, and that to burn such lime nearly four times as much volume of wood is needed as lime produced. Thus every 16 cubic meters of masonry requires about a cord of wood. The lime burning for these structures would have absorbed large labor groups, the size of which has never been estimated, and the number of skilled stonecarvers and stucco-modelers should increase the ratio of skilled to unskilled labor far above the one-fifth proportion estimated for Teotihuacan.

There is much evidence that the transition from the Formative into the Classic stage was gradual in the Maya area. In the Peten region, the center of the Classic Maya calendric developments, the erecting of stone monuments or stelæ bearing carved Maya dates, and the beginnings of the use of the Maya vault, are taken as roughly contemporaneous markers of the beginning of the Classic stage; but in Yucatan, where stelæ are infrequently found, most of the Maya sites which have been archeologically tested show an occupancy lasting from the Formative through the Classic stage with no evidence of a sharp cultural break between them. The decorations of pyramid E VII Sub at Uaxactun suggest that the mask forms so characteristic of Classic symbolic religious art had evolved in Formative times; internal evidence from the Maya calendar also assures us that calendric observations were taken during the last several hundred years of the Formative period, presumably by an organized Maya priesthood.

In summary we can say with some certainty that the tradition of the building of centers for worship, an educated and organized body of Maya priests who used some sort of writing, and an elaborate religious iconography developed during Formative times and reached their greatest complexity during the Classic stage. That these priests also wielded major political powers seems likely; how else can we explain two late Formative tombs at Kaminaljuyu which contained more than 400 pieces of pottery and other elaborate gifts, including the ceremonial mask mentioned above? There is also increasing evidence that the arts and crafts reached full technical competence during late Formative times. Lapidary work of this period was fine, pottery was more carefully made than in later times. The chief technical advances noted for the Classic stage are in writing, religious architecture, and monumental sculpture, arts which were particularly stimulated by institutions developed under the increasingly elaborate and more widely extended social groupings of the Classic stage.

A good archeological summary of the Formative stage in meso America was published in 1950 by Wauchope, Robert, in Middle American Research Records, vol. 1, no. 14, New Orleans. Several articles, particularly those by Longyear, Shook, and Brainerd, in *The Civilization of Ancient America*, Sol Tax editor, Chicago, 1951, give discussions on the Formative stage for various parts of meso America.

III—THE CLASSIC STAGE

Throughout meso America two or three centuries after the time of Christ began a general blossoming out of cultures which continued for the next half millenium. This Classic Stage witnessed the most formally planned religious centers, the most accurate and intricate calendric computations, the most complex and esoteric religious symbolism, the most ornate architecture, and the most sophisticated and mature representational art of aboriginal America. During this span of time the long Formative stage development of technical knowledge bore its flower, this was the golden age of meso America. No short and simple description such as this can encompass its richness and variety; a characteristic development of the period was a congeries of variant cultures, each distinguished by its own peculiar social and religious character, by its own art styles, and by its own particular fields of virtuosity.

On the Mexican mainland the Classic-stage remains show evidence of several strongly integrated art styles, each of which is sharply differentiated from the others, but all of which bear similar elements which must have been a common heritage from the less regionalized Formative stage.

These regions, recognized long before their developments could be anchored chronologically, have been named generally from the tribes of the areas at the time of the Conquest, a usage which is misleading but time-honored. In central Veracruz the Totonac art is characterized by magnificent stone sculptures and ceramics. The site of El Tajin was a major center here in late Classic times. In southern Veracruz and neighboring Tabasco the Olmec art style came to flower with an early and striking style of conventionalized mask. A center here was La Venta. In southern Oaxaca the Zapotec area produced elaborately conventionalized clay figures of gods, well-developed stone masonry and, as in the Olmec area, evidence of written calendrics. The major center here was Monte Alban. In western Mexico the Classic stage as defined here seems to have been weak in development. The Tarascan style of clay modeling and pottery decoration developed along informal, representational lines unrestricted by religious demands so prominent in arts of the other regions. In the Valley of Mexico Teotihuacan is notable for its severe and restrained but handsome paintings, stone sculpture, architecture, and ceramics.

Teotihuacan is notable among these regional centers as the only Classic meso American city thus far identified, the only site where the people lived concentrated about their religious center. This center is oriented along an avenue 206 feet wide upon which front the two huge late Formative pyramids described above. The avenue for a length of a mile and a quarter is lined with temples and other public buildings. Around this center grew up a rabbit warren of contiguous-walled houses over an area of more than three square miles, about seven times the area of the religious center. Scattered through this maze of houses were occasional sunken courtyards lined by four facing porticos on the walls of some of which have been found handsome frescoes which suggest a religious usage for the compounds. The house-plans show intercommunications among rooms in groups of 15 to 30, suggesting that they were occupied by large groups of people living intimately—extended families perhaps. Although there is no evidence for careful planning of the development of residential Teotihuacan, drainage of the site was elaborately arranged by underground conduits faced in stone. With the exception of a few cut-stone faced temple substructures, the most famous of which is called the Ciudadela, the construction of buildings is not monumental but utilitarian; rough stone, mud, wooden posts and beams with lime plaster floors and wall-facings. It has been suggested that the invention of *chinampa* or floating garden agriculture in the waters of Lake Texcoco, coupled with water transport in dugout canoes, permitted food to be supplied in the quantities necessary to sustain a city at this particular locality, and there is some archeological support of this theory. Be this as it may, Teotihuacan seems to be unique in size and population concentration during the Classic stage.

The style of design of the pottery, sculpture, and murals of Teotihuacan is so distinctive that the origin of these objects is recognizable at a glance. The same may be said of the art products of the other regions described. Each of these styles is closely limited, narrow in its conventions, and complex in its organization. The objects are made with consummate skill, arguing for groups of professional craftsmen. The human figures in these styles often wear masks, and these masks, as well as accouterments and certain designs, are repeated in the art of all these regions in such a manner as to suggest that they must have had a symbolic significance to their users, and that many elements of this symbolism were held in common over meso America; several gods must have been widely worshipped. We know also that all meso America used a common religious calendar at the time of European contact, and that this calendar must have been long used; calendric symbols were early carved on stone monuments at Monte Alban and elsewhere.

In addition to the evidence of common origins for the religions of the distinctive Classic cultures, there is much evidence of interchange of luxury goods as well as of art styles between centers. In a temple at Teotihuacan was painted a mural in a style native to the Totonac area. At Kaminaljuyu, Guatemala, the graves of notables contain handsomely decorated objects from central Veracruz, from Teotihuacan, and from the Maya lowlands, and the building techniques used for the tombs are such as to suggest that foremen from Teotihuacan may have directed their construction. In the Maya lowlands Mexican influence was much less, but even here from as far east as British Honduras have been found pottery vessels in Teotihuacan style, and from all parts of the Maya area have come sporadic suggestions of Mexican mainland influence in traded materials, in traded small objects, and through traits in decorative design. Without question this cosmopolitan exchange of goods and ideas over meso America in Classic times was more marked among the ruling priestly classes than among the commoners, but on the Mexican mainland it was never easy enough to allow the fusion of human products into a single style.

The Maya area constitutes roughly the southeastern half of the meso American area. It is but slightly smaller than the Mexican mainland area of high culture and shows throughout a greater degree of cultural homogeneity than does the Mexican mainland. It is usually divided for descriptive purposes into three areas: northern, central, and southern. Of these regions the central area, consisting of the low, heavily forested land of northern Guatemala, British Honduras, and parts of the Mexican states of Tabasco and Chiapas, is the home of the typical Classic Maya development of stone architecture and calendrics. The central Maya area is a long belt of land, which extends in a northwesterly direction from the most southeastern Maya site, Copan, to the most western, Palenque. The earliest Classic Maya calendric and architectural developments have been found at the approximate center of this area in the department of Peten, Guatemala, and gradually extended in both directions through time.

The southern or highland part of the Maya area shows but

little archeological evidence of the unique Maya Classic traits mentioned above, and the linguistic diversity of the area, which shows islands of peoples speaking languages of non-Maya relationship, suggests a chequered history. This mountainous area is penetrated from the north by valleys which show strong Maya developments, notably in ceramics, but the archeological remains are quite distinctive, and show as much or more similarity to Mexican mainland materials than they do to Maya. The legendary histories of Guatemala highlands detail, as do those of Yucatan, a conquest by Toltecs from the Valley of Mexico city of Tula impinging at about 1000 A.D. upon a people of Maya religion.

Thus it may be seen that although the Guatemalan-Salvadoranean highland area has traditionally been placed as part of the Maya area, such placement should be qualified by both archeological and linguistic evidence of Mexican highland influence at various periods, beginning at an early time. Maya material culture, as distinguishable archeologically, seems to hold to the lowlands, possibly due to a lack of economic adaptability of its bearers to the highlands. These highlanders, linked by similarity of their environment to the Mexicans to their north, must have shared many non-material culture traits with the closer and more culturally advanced lowland Maya. It is thought by some that agriculture came to the Maya area from this highland area, and the recognition of a very advanced Formative culture here also suggests early importance of the highlands.

The cultural developments of the Northern Maya area were originally thought to have occurred late in history, after the abandonment of the central Maya area, but recent excavations have shown this concept to have been in error; that Yucatan was well settled and advanced in culture from the Formative stage onward. During Formative times the ceramics of Yucatan are more similar to those of the central Maya area than are highland ceramics; in fact throughout the Classic stage the northern area may be considered relatively free from outside influence, doubtless due to its geographic position.

The northern area itself may be divided into several regions. In Quintana Roo, in areas which form a geographic extension of the Peten rain forest, are sites such as Coba which in all essentials bore Central Maya Classic stage culture. In southwestern Yucatan the hilly Puuc area, and the respectively adjoining Chenes and Rio Bec areas to the south in Campeche and western Quintana Roo seem to have been the seat of architectural and ceramic styles which came to dominate all of Yucatan in late Classic times. This region abuts to the south on typical Central Maya area sites in such a manner as to suggest a political boundary of some sort approximately on the present-day Guatemala-Mexico frontier. These neighboring cultural zones are separated by no marked geographic or physiographic barrier, unless it be that of increasing dryness of climate to the north, coupled with a rather gradual lessening in height of vegetation. The vegetative change from "high bush" to the low bush characteristic of Yucatan now occurs well north of the Peten-Rio Bec cultural boundary; as to whether this was always true we do not know. Northern Yucatan seems to have borne a distinctive culture of its own during early Classic times which shared the Formative traditions carried on in the Peten area. Later this was overwhelmed by the intrusion of the locally developed culture of the Puuc area. In late Classic times there is much evidence of Puuc culture expansion, and evidence of decreasing contact with the Peten to the south. Thus the archeological evidence is clearly against a northward migration of the Central Maya peoples as their area was abandoned. The famous Maya-style ruins of Yucatan, such as Uxmal, Kabah, Labna, Sayil, and Maya Chichen Itza seem to stem from the culture of the Puuc-Chenes-Rio Bec area—they certainly do not represent a renaissance of the central Maya civilization.

The homogeneity of the lowland Maya area is strikingly demonstrated in the style of the Maya calendric monuments on which a recent study (Proskouriakoff 1950) has shown that it is possible to estimate stylistically the date of stelæ within 80 years of the 550 year span with more than 90 percent accuracy, no matter from what part of the central Maya area they come; and this accuracy can be reached in spite of the extremely conservative nature of the composition of the design on these monuments. For more than 500 years the Maya carved similarly clad and positioned human figures on their stelæ. Mannerisms of carving monuments diffused so rapidly in the Maya area that it is difficult not to believe that the artists traveled frequently from center to center. This homogeneity extends, although in a less striking manner, into other human products and makes possible a listing of traits which characterize the Classic Maya culture. Distinctive traits have recently been listed by Morley (1946) for this area: the hieroglyphic writing with its associated calendrics, and the stone-and-mortar architecture with the Maya vault. To these traits could advantageously be added qualifiers and many additions. The calendrics in their turn rest upon sustained and carefully recorded astronomic observations, the systematizing and periodic arranging of which must have required an impressive development of abstract mathematics. A further development of the central Maya area was the perfection of the finest naturalistic art in the New World. The parent of Maya naturalistic art is the much wider spread and earlier symbolic art of the Maya and other meso Americans. It is difficult to assess the iconography of a nearly vanished religion, but the extreme complexity and ordered beauty of Maya symbolic art suggests that in the realm of religious thought the Maya were again supreme in the New World.

The remarkable traits of the Maya culture are of an intellectual and of an esthetic order. Other people excelled them in numerous materialistic fields, the Central Mexicans and Peruvians, for example, in size of structures and in scale and degree of political organization. We know of no proficiency among the Maya in such agricultural techniques as irrigation and fertilization; most advanced agricultural techniques are unavailing in the type of terrain occupied by the Maya. Although it is possible that, through some agricultural system unknown to us, the Maya may have attained a high population density, it does not seem that the assumption of such a density is necessary to account for the manpower used in architectural construction. Maya construction is not notable for its size, but is unique, at least in the New World, for its evidence of craftsmanship. The population need not have been heavy, but if not, it must have contained an extraordinarily high proportion of skilled artisans. This suggests an emphasis on quality rather than on quantity, on enlightenment rather than on power in the code of Maya values.

For a general discussion of the Classic stage, see Kidder, Jennings and Shook, *Excavations at Kaminaljuyu, Guatemala*, pp. 1-9, 241-260, Washington 1946. For regional art styles of the Classic stage, see T. A. Joyce, *Maya and Mexican Art*, London 1927, and Pal Kelemen, *Medieval American Art*, v. 2, New York, 1944. For regional developments in the Northern and Southern Maya area, see J. E. S. Thompson in *American Antiquity*, 9: 106-134 and 11: 2-24, Menasha, Wis.

ARCHITECTURE

The architectural remains of the Classic stage Maya are found in groups, each of which undoubtedly was a center of religious worship supported by the people of the surrounding countryside. The architectural groups are often, though not invariably, found on high ground. The low ridge or peak bearing the architectural group or groups has usually been leveled to form flat plazas or courtyards which were bounded by stone-faced, sloped retaining walls, underlaid where necessary with stone, or occasionally with earth fill, and floored in lime plaster. These plazas range from very small up to 150 yards or more square. Their shape is generally rectangular, sometimes varied by neighboring plazas, the terrain, or buildings which impinge on them, and they are often connected by carefully built causeways (Map II).

Along the edges of the plazas, and sometimes in their centers, were built structures of stone masonry. These have been classified into two general types: "temples" and "palaces".

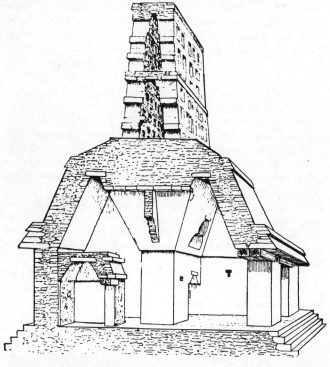

FIG. 5—TEMPLE OF THE CROSS, PALENQUE. TRANSVERSE SECTION AND PERSPECTIVE. This temple rests on a high stepped pyramid. Note the battered upper wall zone, the hollow roof comb. The Palenque temples are the most elaborate, as well as the most lightly constructed masonry temples of the Maya area. (Drawing by W. H. Holmes)

These terms are unfortunate but long established; the temples were likely used as such, the use of the palaces is not known accurately, and they do not form a closely definable type. Temples (fig. 5) are small buildings having from one to four rooms arranged on a single story; they characteristically surmount a tall solid, masonry-faced substructure in the form of a stepped pyramid with one or more steep staircases ascending it. The palaces are in general characterized by larger and more complex floor plans, and by a low substructure which is often no more than a plinth. A few generalizations may be made as to their plans. Rooms are arrayed in linear ranges, and all doorways open outward onto a frontal platform. Multistoried buildings have ranges of rooms surrounding a solid core and each story is set back so that it overlies a portion of the core. Most vaulted temples and many palace type buildings are surmounted by roof combs, tall masonry structures designed to ornament and to make more imposing the squarish building beneath them. Roof combs are often hollow, with reticulated walls for lightness, and are usually built over a heavy central wall for maximum stability.

Maya stone masonry differs from that of other parts of the New World most strikingly in its use of lime mortar. Cut stone masonry was extensively employed on the Mexican mainland, and more massive and carefully cut masonry was made in Peru than was ever employed by the Maya, but lime mortar was not characteristically used in laying masonry in either of those areas although it was used at various times and places for wall and floor facing. The mortar used in the Maya area may have hardened with time in Maya buildings; today many of them are monolithic in structure, the mortar often is harder than the stone. Maya mortar consists of slaked lime mixed with from one and one-half to four parts of a powdery lime breccia which performs the function of silica sand which does not occur in most of the Maya area. There is evidence that Maya mortar floors were impregnated with an organic solution to harden and color the surface.

The planning and layout of Maya buildings varies somewhat by time period and area but the following generalizations can be made.

Wall lines are normally straight; vertical walls are plumb, and battered walls quite constant in slope. Exact right angles, however, are seldom found. Thus it would seem that lines were stretched, and plumb lines held in wall construction, but that no method for laying out right angles was employed. Wall plans have been found scratched into floors, and the symmetry and proportion of buildings and assemblages makes it nearly certain that plans or models were made before construction. Although the elaborate building plans, and exact duplication of architectural decorative elements in Maya buildings suggest that units of measure must have been used in planning and construction, I know of no attempts made thus far to discover them.

The orientation of buildings and plazas is rather constant within sites, but varies more widely between sites. In general, the sides of buildings and plazas tend to be oriented with the cardinal directions. In sites of the central Maya area during the early Classic stage a type of group arrangement with possible astronomical significance is found at a number of sites. Three small buildings are placed along the east side of a plaza, usually all three resting on a low substructure. On the west side of the same plaza is placed a single tall pyramid which does not bear a temple. Since we know from pre Conquest manuscripts that astronomical sightings were taken from pyramids it is possible that these groups allowed the direct observation of the sun at equinox and solstices.

The stones used in Maya walls normally show sign of shaping and surfacing by means of pecking with a hard stone hammer, and in the finest examples exposed faces were pecked to toothed but remarkably flat surfaces. The quality of finish varies with the character of stone used. Limestone preponderates, and varies from soft material of poor cleavage to a fine textured, homogeneous almost marble-like quality. Hammerstones seem to have been usually made of the flinty concretions found in the limestone. No metal tools were used in stone working before the European conquest. The masonry seems to have been invariably covered with lime mortar, either thin or thick; the mortar was normally given a polished surface and often painted in brilliant colors. The wall stones are usually coursed horizontally and have a variable amount of tenoning into the wall interior. No regular intentional off-setting of joints between neighboring courses is found, nor were adjoining walls usually intentionally bonded by offset joints at building corners, a peculiar lack, considering the excellence of the stone masonry in other regards. Size of stone elements used in walls is almost always small, of such size that a man could carry the stone. Exceptions to this rule are the stone stelæ, door jambs and lintels, and molding stones which are characteristically set at the spring of the vault. All of these were necessarily larger due to the requirements of their use.

Three types of roofing are known from the Maya sites, thatch, beam-and-mortar, and corbel vault. Thatch roofs are known from modern Maya houses and from drawings and sculpture of the Classic stage. Such roofing was likely the earliest type used in the area, and is still the commonest type; thatch roofs are widespread over the New World. They were fitted to wooden truss work which was fastened by the use of the crotches of the timbers and by bindings of tropical vines. Although archeological identification of such roofs is difficult, and it is known that they were not used on the more important of the Classic Maya buildings, their depiction in Maya art, the widespread modern use of structurally similar roofs of this type, its finely drawn functional development, and the elaborate Maya nomenclature for roof-parts attests a long history for the thatched roof in the Maya area.

Beam-and-mortar roofs also have a wide distribution over the New World. There is archeological evidence of their use during the Classic and following stages in the Maya area in the buildings of the religious centers, and they were in use on the homes of the wealthier people at the time of the Spanish Conquest. At Tulum, a late post Classic site on the eastern Yucatan coast, a beamed roof was found in place. Heavy squared beams span the rooms. On these, at right angle, was placed a continuous layer of smaller unhewn beams, which was in turn surmounted by a mixture of small stones and mortar to make a thick, impervious cap, sloped on the top for drainage. The survival of such mortar caps at Tulum shows that they had become monolithic, bearing their own weight independently of the supporting beams. Modern Yucatecan beamed roofs are often jack vaulted between wooden beams, nearly certainly a European innovation. Although it is often impossible to distinguish archeologically between beam-and-mortar and thatch roofed structures, it can be said that neither type was used on the more important buildings of the Classic stage in the Central Maya area, but that they were used for major temples in Yucatan during post Classic times, their prominence at that time doubtless due to influence from the Mexican mainland. In the Maya region of the Guatemala highlands thatch, and beam-and-mortar roofs were universal during all periods.

The corbeled vault was the roof *par excellence* of the Classic Maya. It is limited to the Maya in meso America; although it occurred over a wide area in the South American Andes it seems to have been limited there to use as a substitute for scarce wood, and was held to a primarily functional purpose rather than developed as an architectural glory. The strength of corbeled vaulting theoretically depends upon the principle of the cantilever; the two sides of each vault are built separately, each half vault usually balanced upon its supporting wall. Stone vault slabs are laid, each successively projecting a bit farther inward from the inner face of the wall, and each at the same time held in place by other stones which carry the outer face of the wall vertically upward. The result in section is an inverted right triangle, the hypotenuse of which forms the vault soffit. The center of gravity of this mass of masonry must lie vertically above the supporting wall if it is to balance thereon, and this requires a heavy mass of vault masonry vertically above the supporting wall, bonded to, and counterbalancing the masonry of the vault face. The two vault halves are usually bridged at their adjoining edges by a series of flat, thin slabs, and the whole is topped by a faintly domed layer of mortar for weather proofing. These are the technical specifications.

In practice the Maya in certain of their more elaborate buildings sometimes deviated by sloping the outer face of the vault inward. This procedure, which produces a "mansard roof" shaped exterior lightens the weight of the vault, thus relieving vertical stress on the building walls (fig. 5). It throws the center of gravity of the vault mass farther into the room than the inner edge of the walls, however, necessitating that the two halves of the vault support each other at the apex, and additionally it exerts an outward push on the tops of the sidewalls, which must be met, since the Maya used no buttresses, either by thick sidewalls, or by room end walls bonded to the sidewalls. Since masonry corner bonding was poorly understood among the Maya, this solution was at best insufficient. To support these unbalanced vault halves before the construction had proceeded far enough for them to meet, the Maya used horizontal beams which were set into the sides of the facing vault halves, and left in place after finishing. They may also have used vertical supports of wood under the vault during building.

Further departures from architectural functionalism in Maya vaulting were made possible by their ability to produce huge monolithic masses of masonry by the use of quantities of lime mortar. The majority of Maya vaults must have depended upon wooden beaming and scaffolding during construction, or at the least upon a succession of halts in construction (often detectable even now in the masonry) to allow the mortar to set to a monolithic mass capable of supporting the next building stage. Actually holes for scaffold-beams are found nearly universally in Maya vaults. It should be emphasized that Maya masonry construction is anything but economical in materials and time for the useful space obtained. An extreme example of this lack of functionalism is found in the Tikal temples where about seven-eighths of the floor space is occupied by masonry walls. These were a sacrifice to make possible the support of the imposing but tremendously heavy roof-comb, just as the huge underlying pyramids were of use only to raise the temple above the worshippers in the plaza.

Aside from the plazas and the two types of buildings described above, the Classic Maya built a variety of specialized constructions. Among these are ball courts, maze-like galleries enclosed in masonry structures, sweatbaths, portal-vaults at entrances to architectural groups, ceremonial platforms, vaulted bridges, causeways. Ball courts consist of two facing, parallel masses of masonry between which a game was played with a large, solid rubber ball. Some courts have small stone rings mounted vertically on the sidewalls of the court; many courts have further masonry walls which delimit a playing area in form of an I. This ball game was played, as shown by remains of the courts, from well south of the Maya area in Salvador as far north as central Arizona. The sweatbath has a nearly universal New World distribution; the Maya buildings are of vaulted masonry with a room with small, low doorway, and a channel for disposal of the hot water used. Portal-vaults are open at both ends for use as entrances to plazas, and are often short in proportion to span and height. Ceremonial platforms are low, paved structures built in the centers of plazas very similar to those used for dances by the Aztecs at the time of the Conquest. Causeways linked plazas within ruins, and sometimes ran between ruins at some distances. The longest yet discovered, between Coba and Yaxuna in the northeast part of the Yucatan peninsula, is about 120 kilometers long. There are probably many more causeways in existence than those which have been traced. The causeways are built of rough limestone, averaging perhaps 15 meters wide; they probably had plastered surfaces. Often a border of large limestone slabs flanks the causeway to either side. These roads run very straight, ascending rises in the ground, and running over masonry fill when the ground is low. Small sanctuaries are found to the sides of them, some containing stelae. A heavy stone cylinder. used as a road roller, was found on the Yaxuna-Coba causeway. It seems very questionable that such roads were necessary for transportation. The Maya had neither wheeled vehicles nor organized armies, and trails should have taken care of all foot traffic with ease. It has been suggested that the causeways may have been built for religious processions. The presence of these causeways is one of our best evidence for governmental unity over more than the environs of simple religious centers. Unquestionably close cooperation between the governments of the sites concerned would have been necessary for their building and upkeep, and this problem would have been immeasurably easier if a common government had ruled the religious centers.

CHRONOLOGICAL AND REGIONAL VARIATION

Several trends in building techniques are observable in the history of the central Maya area during Classic times. The earliest masonry consists of unshaped or very roughly shaped blocks set uncoursed in a heavy bed of mortar, often wedged with rough stone spalls (fig. 6a). Walls are evened up with a thick coat of mortar, and architectural decoration when present is modeled in mortar (stucco) with minimum amount of support from projecting, crude stone elements.

Vaults are also built of rough slabs, which are laid horizontally or with an upward slope toward the interior and evened, as are the walls, with an extravagant quantity of mortar (fig. 6b). The spring of the vault was usually marked in these times by a row of large slabs which go clear through the wall to form a bearing surface for the vault and a projecting medial cornice on the exterior. Most buildings were of the temple type, each isolated on its substructure, several facing upon a single plaza.

Changes from these characteristics are noted at Uaxactum walls beginning at about 9.8.0.0.0. (ca 600 A.D.) by the beginnings of Central Maya style veneer masonry (fig. 6c). The later building walls are made with cores of rough, unworked stone and mortar faced on the outer side by carefully cut, smooth faced, "veneer" stones, more or less rectangular in shape with smoothly pecked outer faces. These stones

were coursed and set with reasonable precision, their backs set
into the rich mortar of the core and sometimes bonded to it
with carefully spaced headers. The core itself was monolithic,
that is self supporting after hardening, and standing buildings
are often seen which have lost their smooth stone veneer but
remain solid. Interior wall faces were at first evened by a
heavy mortar coat as in the earlier period, later they were
veneered with smooth masonry. The vaults of the later period
underwent essentially the same changes as did the walls. The
latest vault stones were block shaped with a face beveled to the
soffit slope. They were coursed, and tailed deeply into the
monolithic hearting. The cornice stones of the later buildings
do not project through the whole wall thickness but are deeply
tailed.   In general there was a tendency for the temple type to

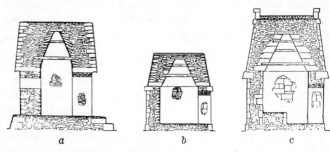

a   *b*   *c*

FIG. 6—TRANSVERSE SECTIONS OF BUILDINGS AT UAXACTUN, GUATEMALA.
These sections show typical masonry construction; to the left is early
Classic, center is transitional, right late Classic, all from the central Maya
area. (Drawings by A. L. Smith)

give way in popularity to place-type buildings, long ranges of
rooms often bordering the sides of rectangular plazas. Although the Maya continued to cover all wall surfaces with
stucco, the smoother faces of later masonry allowed the use of
a thin plaster coat. Heavy, elaborately modeled stucco ornament continued to be used through the Classic stage in the central Maya area, supplemented at such sites as Copan by stone
sculpture in the round, and at Palenque by low relief sculpture.
The bas-relief panels are usually made of a single slab, and
sculptures in the round are either carved from single blocks
or from a few large blocks.
     Several regions of the central Maya area show evidence of
superlative local developments in architecture during the
Classic stage. The architecture of Copan to the extreme
southeast of the Maya area is a case in point, as is the archi-

tecture of Palenque to the west. The stelae dates of these two
sites, and of others in their areas, begin later in time than
those of the central Peten. Initial series dated monuments
thus seem to have been originated in the Peten and this custom
must have diffused from there, but this fact provides no
certain evidence as to the origin of architectural or other
cultural advances within the Maya area. The origins of other
Maya arts and techniques are much more difficult to trace,
and the familiar theory that the Peten Maya area was a
center from which other areas developed provincially is still
unproved. Our knowledge of Formative development suggests
more highly developed centers in Highland Guatemala, Northwest Honduras, and perhaps in the La Venta area and Yucatan
than in the Peten, although our sampling during this period
is so spotty that it is of uncertain value. It also cannot be said
at present that the earliest vaults come from the Peten, but
only that the earliest vaults which have been dated by Maya
inscriptions come from there. And whatever can eventually
be said as to the differences in regional development within
the Maya area, the final picture is more likely to be that of a
culturally unified area, each region of which had its
special styles and cultural achievements, than that of a center
of culture from which all blessings flowed with force diminishing as the distance from the Peten "center" increased.

Yucatan has its own well-known and distinctive architecture which dates from late Classic and post Classic
times. In recent years it has become evident, however, that
early Classic period architecture, of a type close to that of the
central Maya area, also exists in Yucatan, often built over or
obscured by the great number of better preserved later buildings. These old sites often, but not always, contain carved
and plain stelæ. The earliest dated architecture in Yucatan
is at Oxkintok where it is with reasonable certainty associated
with an inscription (reading 9.2.0.0.0, 475 A.D.) and with
pottery of the early Classic period. The buildings at Oxkintok,
and certain other undated buildings in Yucatan, are very close
in form and masonry to those of the central area.

The Rio Bec and Chenes areas, which lie between Yucatan
and the Peten, show architecture in which the masonry construction is not far from Classic veneer masonry of the Peten,
although in the Chenes area the block-shape veneer stones are
much more finely cut and finished than those in the Peten,
and the vault stones are better cut, probably due to the fine
quality of the local limestone. The planning of the sites, and

the form and decoration of buildings, however, are highly distinctive, and in general closer to that of the Puuc area than to that of the Peten area. The architecture of the Puuc area is outstanding in quality and quite distinctive in structural technique. It is also of the veneer type, composed of carefully cut stone facings covering a monolithic stone-and-mortar core. It differs from Peten veneer masonry in that the facing stones are relatively thinner, and are beveled toward the interior so that the mortar bonding extends from the core between the beveled facing stones almost to the wall surface (fig. 7). The veneer stones are thus in the form of truncated pyramids with carefully smoothed bases rather than of block-shape as those of the Peten. A some-

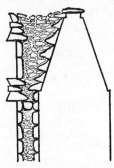

FIG. 7—TRANSVERSE SECTION OF BUILDING AT UXMAL, YUCATAN, SHOWING TYPICAL PUUC REGION VENEER MASONRY CONSTRUCTION. (Drawing by A. L. Smith)

what parallel distinction is evident in the facing stones of Puuc vaulting. These stones are also beveled, or tapered to allow a deep mortar bond, and the finely finished face is sloped to fit the vault soffit. The depth of Puuc vault-stones varies from shallow, as are the wall stones, to deeply tongued stones often characterized as of "boot-shape." The shallowest of these vault-stones must have been supported by forms when laid; both wall- and vault-stones have often fallen, leaving a core covered with meshwork of raised mortar ridges which originally supported the surface masonry.

The architecture of the Puuc, Rio Bec, and Chenes areas has much in common. In all this area Initial Series dates are all but lacking, as are in general the stelæ which bore them. Site arrangements tend to be less compact and more irregular than in the Peten. The quadrangle, a rectangular plaza surrounded by ranges of rooms, is common through the area. Walls of buildings are markedly thinner in proportion to room size. Decoration by means of mosaic-like panels or zones composed of many carved blocks tenoned into the core is universal, but shows marked regional variation. In the Rio Bec area decoration is often in the form of huge, very conventionalized serpent-heads arranged with a door as the mouth, and the stones are crude, meant for a heavy stucco coat. In the Puuc area alone the decoration is usually limited to the upper

FIG. 8.—PORTAL VAULT AT LABNA, YUCATAN (PUUC REGION). Lower wall, zones are of carefully cut veneer masonry. Note the Maya thatched-roof houses sculptured on this facade. (T. A. Willard photo)

FIG. 9—FACADE AT SAYIL, YUCATAN. The round columns used as door-lintel supports, and the mosaic-mask decorations are typical of the Puuc region. (T. A. Willard photo)

wall panels, and is carefully carved to need a minimum of
stucco (fig. 8). Decorated areas are usually in the form of
panels in the Chenes and Rio Bec areas, whereas in the Puuc,
whole upper wall zones are decorated. wide doorways divided
by a central round column are common to the north, rare to
the south (fig. 9). All three areas are characterized by large
multistoried palaces, which in the Chenes and Rio Bec areas
are often ornamented with towers made in the form of tall,
narrow pyramids topped by dummy temples.

The reconstruction of the history of these transitional
regions between the central and northern Maya areas is difficult
at present but my present hypothesis, based largely on un-
published and as yet incompletely analyzed ceramic material,
is that somewhere in the Puuc-Chenes-Rio Bec area a
culture distinctive in both architecture and ceramics differentiated out of the underlying Maya culture pattern. This
process probably began at the beginning of the ninth Maya
calendric cycle or earlier. This culture was characterized by
slateware pottery as well as by the architectural traits noted
above. The culture spread, encountering central Maya culture
to the south, and the hitherto nearly unpopulated and dry but
agriculturally rich area of the Puuc hills to the north. The
Puuc area was populated by the development of a cistern
system (the chultunes) used for drinking water during the
dry season, and became the culture center at nearly the end of
the ninth cycle (about 800 A.D.). From here the Puuc culture
spread throughout Yucatan until transformed by the Toltec
invasion at, or somewhat after, the end of the Classic stage.

For comparative meso American architecture see Ignacio
Marquina, *Arquitectura Prehispanica*, Mexico, 1951. For Classic
Maya architecture see A. P. Maudslay in *Biologia Centrali-
Americana*, sections on archeology, London, 1889-1902; G. O.
Totten, *Maya Architecture*, Washington, 1926; T. Proskouria-
koff, *An Album of Maya Architecture*, Washington, 1946; A. L.
Smith, *Uaxactun, Guatemala: Excavations of 1931-1937*, Wash-
ington, 1950. For modern Maya housing see Robert Wauchope,
Modern Maya Houses, Washington, 1938.

RELIGION

Maya art, Maya architecture, and most formal aspects of
Classic Maya life were religiously oriented. The Maya gods
from our knowledge of the hieroglyphs were characterized by
certain facial peculiarities and special regalia (fig. 10). They
were considered as guardians of time-periods as well as of parts
of the Maya cosmos. They were generally conceived in groups
of four which might be subsumed in one, a conception not

unlike that of the Christian trinity, save that the Maya concept is linked with the four cardinal directions. The Maya also believed in duality of gods, each having a good and evil aspect linked respectively with the sky and underworld. There were also gods who were patrons of occupations; these may have been specialized versions of more generally worshipped deities.

The style of Maya and Mexican mainland religions is very similar, indeed the similarities in many cases are so close as to include transliterated names of gods. The great complexity and confusion among the fully developed regional religions of meso America may be assumed to have been caused by the superimposing of increasingly elaborated regional concepts, the introduction of new gods, and shifts in emphasis and attributes

FIG. 10—MAYA GODS AS SHOWN IN THE DRESDEN CODEX. The Sun God, the Death God, and the Jaguar God.

of others, upon a simple agricultural pantheon of earth, rain, and sky gods which must have been universal in the Formative stage. Illuminating parallels to this shifting situation may be found in the better documented histories of the early Mesopotamian and Egyptian religions.

The dependence on gods for agricultural yield and the offering of a round of sacrifices to propitiate them is practically as widespread in the New World as is agriculture itself. To this round of sacrifices were geared the meso American calendrics and their associated astronomy, and a system of ceremonies and sacrifices of ever-increasing complexity, as well as the development of astrological forecasting. The Maya religious centers and perhaps the Aztec cult of human sacrifice may be considered as the culminating stages of this development. None of these elaborately ramified institutions seems to have had a direct utility in the economic life of the people who were dominated by them, although Maya economy could well have supported such frills; it has been calculated that the modern Maya can make a living for his family on only fifty days of agricultural work per year.

Economic motives and controls which could have effectively welded together Maya groups to permit the construction of the huge and elaborate architectural centers are difficult to fathom. In the earliest Old World civilizations the growth of organized political power has been explained by the control of irrigation rights by priestly classes in Mesopotamia and by the ability to predict the Nile floods held by a calendrically-minded group of priests in Egypt. In fact the concentrated dwelling patterns themselves in these regions, made economically advisable by the rich land yields of multiple crop irrigation, have been suggested as a major aid to close political control. An effort has been made to apply these same theories of economic determinism for the New World, where in Peru and in the parts of the Mexican mainland where irrigation was practised they can be made to fit. The Maya area, with its slash-burn agriculture, and its archeological evidence that during the Classic stage as now the people must have been distributed in a diffuse settlement pattern, presents a different problem. Although the priests may have been effective in making agriculturally valuable weather forecasts, this function hardly seems enough to have accounted for their unquestioned control over large groups of people.

The Maya area is a large exception to be permitted in a theoretical scheme which aims at explaining the universal factors in the growth of civilization. Other possibly important New World exceptions may be ceramically rich cultures known from the mouth of the Amazon, and the Woodland cultures of eastern United States, recently shown by radioactive carbon dates to have been much earlier in developing than previously supposed. One may wonder if the chances of archeological sampling may not have influenced our concepts of the development of civilization, and that the fact that most of the known evidence of early civilization in the world comes from dry areas, may not be due to the fact that remains are better preserved and easier to locate in such areas. Only archeological surveys in warm wet areas can settle this point.

This has been a fruitless search for an economic impetus which started the Maya in their expanding preoccupation with religious ceremonialism and on their path to outstanding cultural development. Perhaps no stern economic control was necessary; originality of thought is not normally the fruit of regimentation. If the Maya did not need vast supplies of manpower for their public works, and had time free from gaining a livelihood, and if, as the evidence suggests, their religion was more complex than their economy, economic factors may not have been those which sparked their cultural florescence. Advances in non-material fields are hard to assess by archeological methods, but we can recognize even with our limited evidence remarkable Maya discoveries in mathematics and astronomy. It seems as though in the case of the Maya intellectual enlightenment it may not have been accomplished nor immediately preceded by the invention of new techniques for economic betterment. Whatever may be the causes behind the unique Maya intellectual progress, they do not fit easily into the sequences of advancement worked out for other early civilizations. This suggests that we do not yet understand fully the factors which lead a people to intellectual progress. These factors would be valuable to know! And of course the fate of Maya culture may also allow generalizations as to the results of abstract, uneconomically directed intellectual progress on the political fortunes of a human group.

For further information on Maya religion see J. Eric S. Thompson, *Maya Hieroglyphic Writing. Introduction.* Washington, 1950.

CALENDRICS

Maya calendrics, as well as Maya religion under which they were developed, are shared in a diluted degree with the rest of meso America, but, at least from Classic times when we first know them, their focus of highest development was the central Maya area.

As has been pointed out above, there is some reason to suspect that the Maya believed that time itself was cyclical or repetitive in nature; their calendrics were certainly organized on this principle. The Maya calendric system may be visualized as a sort of gear box of meshing calendars, a set of gears representing each separate calendar, all interarticulated with each other. The calendric results can be likened to the reading of a gas meter, or of the recording part of an automobile speedometer, save that the separate figures (digits) read from these meters all stand in decimal (one to ten) relationship to each other, whereas most of the Maya calendric counts are not direct multiples of each other, and several are not even factorable. These non-factorable cycles are necessary in all calendars which deal with days and solar years, which themselves are not multiples of each other.

The most widespread, and thus probably the oldest, of these calendars is the sacred calendar or *tzolkin*. The days of this calendar were always noted by a day-name, preceded by a number (or coefficient). Thirteen numbers are used and twenty day names, thus allowing 260 distinctive day designations before the calendar begins to repeat itself. These numbers and day names are ordered like the teeth of two meshed gears—one with 20 teeth, one with 13, or in a manner analogous to the way in which our days of the week, and days within the month, are ordered as shown in the following table:

Tzolkin dates in sequence				*Our week days and month days*					
1 Ik	6 Manik	11 Eb	3 Caban	Mon.	1	Sat.	6	Tues.	30
2 Akbal	7 Lamat	12 Ben	4 Eznab	Tues.	2	Sun.	7	Wed.	1
3 Kan	8 Muluc	13 Ix	5 Cauac	Wed.	3	Mon.	8	Thurs.	2
4 Chicchan	9 Oc	1 Men	6 Ahau	Thurs.	4	....		Fri.	3
5 Cimi	10 Chuen	2 Cib	7 Imix	Fri.	5	....		Sat.	4

The reason why the peoples of meso America settled on 260 days as the length of their religious calendar is not known. This length bears no relationship to astronomical constants. It is, however, rather close to the average length of the agricultural growing season in meso America, and thus could give an indication of the length of time from sowing to harvesting, but its lack of connection with the solar calendar must have been a grave inconvenience. The use of 20 day names coincides with all of the Maya arithmetical usage that we know; the Maya worked in a vigesimal system. The original number 20 may have come from a habit of counting on fingers and toes. The original choice of the cycle of 13 numbers is difficult to justify, but we know that the named days were considered as gods and thus the use of 13 may trace from an already crystallized pantheon. And most certainly a major ritual use of the calendar must have been to order the sacrifices during the growing season. Used thus it would allow couples of gods, one from the number, one from the name of the day, to be worshipped in round-robin fashion.

The *vague year* is a time period of 365 days, uncorrected by periodic leap years. It was used in conjunction with the sacred calendar over much of meso America. This year has been called the *haab*, probably erroneously, by various authors on Maya calendrics. The vague year was divided into 18 named "months" of 20 numbered days each, and a final month of

five days. The Maya numbered the days of the month from
zero to 19, but used them in relation to elapsed time rather
than current time so that their zero day of a month is equiva-
lent to our first day. The vague year calendar is not a com-
bination of two cyclically repeating sequences of unequal numbers of days as is the sacred calendar, but is, as is our calendar,
an organized system for subdividing a significant period of
time, the solar year, rounded to its nearest day. Dates of this
calendar were written in the same fashion as those of the
sacred calendar, with a numerical coefficient followed by a
name glyph. In the sacred calendar the glyph stands for a day,
in the vague year calendar it stands for a month. This is
analogous to our system of the division of the Julian year into
named months of necessarily unequal duration, which in turn
are composed of numbered days.

On the Maya monuments of the Classic stage, the inscriptions usually contain notations of the position of a day in
each of the above two calendars. A day so described is fixed
in cyclic position within a much longer time span than if
written in either of the above calendars alone. 260 and 365,
the days in each of the respective calendars, are factorable by
five. Therefore the length of this composite cycle after which
the complete day designation repeats itself equals $\frac{260 \times 365}{5} = 18,$-
980 days or about 52 solar years. This 52 year period is called
the calendar round. There is no evidence to suggest that this
52 year cycle was considered of religious significance among
the Maya, but the Aztecs wrote their histories with this time
span as a maximum measure of time, analogous to our century. Believing that at the end of each cycle the gods reëx-
amined human conduct, the Aztecs did penance for sins of
the past, destroyed old objects, and prayed the gods for a
world renewal before the beginning of each new cycle.

The component calendars of the calendar round were probably nearly universally used in meso America during the Classic stage, they have been found still in use in several variants
in mountain villages in Guatemala and southern Mexico.

The *long count* consists of a reckoning of the number of
days elapsed since the beginning of the Maya era. It is characteristic of the central part of the Maya area during the Classic stage. It has been commonly assumed to have been invented
in the Peten area, because the earliest long count inscriptions
thus far decipherable are found there. In a much later astronomic manuscript (the Dresden codex) lunar observations
dating back nearly 160 years earlier than the earliest known

inscriptions are recorded. Inscriptions without glyphs, but with the same type of numeral as have the Maya dates, have been found at Tres Zapotes and other sites at the southwest corner of the Gulf of Mexico, some of which, if they have been read correctly and if the same long count can be assumed to have been used in the two areas, date earlier than the earliest Maya dates. Thus it is possible that the long count may have originated in this (the Olmec or La Venta) area. Since both the form of dating and position of starting dates are unknown from the La Venta area, these inscriptions remain interesting but uncertain until more chronologic evidence from this area is available.

The long count must have been invented to allow the more accurate recording of long periods of time. The interest of the Maya in time seems to have been amazingly sustained and pervasive. Their monuments were not for the greater part erected to commemorate political events, but to mark the ending of major time periods, and the subject matter of Maya art is not that of political events but of ceremonies and sacrifices which commemorated calendric events. Although the Maya chronicles of the Guatemala highlands of Conquest times describe dynasties and events as do the Mexican highland chronicles, those of Yucatan show even this late a major interest in time, and the fitting of past history as well as of prophesies to the framework of the major Maya time periods.

The development of a positional system of recording numbers made possible the keeping and writing of long counts. Maya arithmetic is notable for its use of positional significance in counting. This system was used only in the Maya and related areas in the New World. It was invented independently and used by the Mesopotamians two millenia before Christ in a somewhat imperfect form, then lost and either reinvented or revived by the medieval Arabic mathematicians from whom we inherit it. The Greeks and Romans, adequate mathematicians in other respects, did not use it and were thereby hindered; compare for example the Roman notation XVIII with Arabic 18 for ease in writing and computing. The principle of positional notation is that a series of named quantities be used, each a constant multiple of that below it in sequence (in our case units, tens, hundreds, etc.), and that large quantities be written by means of groups of numbers, the quantity which each number indicates being shown by its position. For ex-

ample, our number 547 is read 5 hundreds (the quantity one
hundred is indicated by the third place from the right), 4 tens
(tens occupy the second place from the right), and 7 units
(first place from the right). Maya arithmetic numbers begin
with units at the bottom rather than from the right as with
us, and the Maya system was built primarily of twenties (a
vigesimal system), as contrasted with our decimal system. The

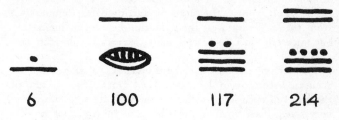

6   100   117   214

FIG. 11—MAYA NUMBERS WITH THEIR ARABIC EQUIVALENTS.

numbers used by the Maya within the positions were: a bar
for five, a dot for one, and a conventionalized shell symbol for
zero (fig. 11). The use of zero, another meso American invention which was unique in the New World, seems to have
preceded the use of zero in the Old World.

The Maya, for purposes of recording dates in their long
count, used multiples of days in a modified vigesimal system
which included the following time periods:

> 20 *kins* (days) make one *uinal*
> 18 *uinals* (20 day months) make one *tun*
> 20 *tuns* (360 day years) make one *katun*
> 20 *katuns* (19.71 years each) make one *baktun*
> 20 *baktuns* (400 *tuns* each) make one *pictun*
> 20 *pictuns* (8000 *tuns*) make one *calabtun*
> 20 *calabtuns* (160,000 *tuns*) make one *Alautun* of 64,000,-
> 000 *tuns*

It will be noted that each of the above time periods contains
20 units of the preceding time period save for the tun which
contains 18 uinals. This deviation was presumably made to
bring the *tun* closer to the solar year (the tun contains 360
days rather than 365.24 days). The long count was written
on the monuments by successive numbers, each applying to
one of the above time periods, in sequence from large to small.
Each of these numbers was additionally accompanied by a

glyph naming its time period. All the dates on Maya monuments, with the exception of a few which we assume were not contemporaneous to their writing, lie within three baktuns; 8, 9, and 10. We normally write these dates as 8. 14. 3. 1. 12, meaning 8 baktuns, 14 katuns, 3 tuns, 1 uinal, and 12 kins. 8. 14. 3. 1. 12. is the earliest long count certainly known, 10. 4. 0. 0. 0 is the latest. Most monuments in this sequence are inscribed with katun ending dates: 9. 16. 0. 0. 0. The long count inscriptions thus cover a period of 589 years, during which dates are documented to the day.

When long count inscriptions appear on monuments they are usually preceded by a characteristic introductory glyph, and followed by a series of glyphs with numerical coefficients which additionally include the calendar round date of the day named by the long count, glyphs which probably give the phase of the moon, and quite often by counts of days running either backward or forward from the long count day. Other glyphs found in these inscriptions have never been deciphered. A whole inscription of this sort is called an Initial Series inscription (fig. 12).

In the Dresden codex, one of the three Maya preconquest books left to us, is a series of elaborate arithmetical counts which give the length in days of the cycle of the planet Venus. In these counts the successive Venus cycles are given each its own slightly varying length in days, thus allowing (as does our leap year sequence) a correction for fractional days.

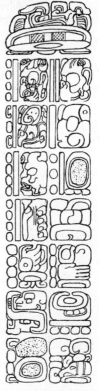

FIG. 12—INITIAL SERIES INSCRIPTION FROM STELA 36, PIEDRAS NEGRAS. The glyphs record (reading left to right by rows): Introducing glyph, 9 baktuns, 10 katuns, 6 tuns, 5 uinals, 9 kins, 8 muluc, 6 glyphs of a supplementary series, 2 Zip. (Drawing by S. G. Morley.)

We know of no direct use of fractions among the Maya. There is also evidence, although it is somewhat dubious, that the Maya recorded the occurrence of eclipses.

There is good internal evidence from the calendrics that although the Maya ceased to carve their long count inscriptions at the Maya date of 10. 4. 0. 0. 0, the count of days continued to be kept until the Conquest, that the katun continued in its great ceremonial importance, and that katuns were named and counted by the tzolkin designation of the last day of each. Since the number of days per katun is divisible by 20 (the number of day names used), the final day of each katun always bore the same name, *ahau*. The numerical coefficient of this day ahau, however, changes with each katun, repeating only after the passage of 13 katuns, a time span of 256 ¼ solar years. Katun ending dates were described to the early Spaniards in Yucatan. The calendar was called the *round of the katuns,* and events were dated as occurring, for example, "in a katun 4 ahau", meaning in a katun, the last day of which was a 4 ahau.

Another method of writing dates has been hypothesized by Thompson to account for certain inscriptions found on buildings of Maya style at Chichen Itza. These dates consist of a calendar round, followed by a tun glyph, then by an ahau glyph, each usually with a numerical coefficient. By assuming that the ahau glyph is to be read as the last day of a katun, as was the custom at Conquest times, and that the tun gives the year within the 20 year period (the katun), the dates can be fixed in the Maya long count. This method of reading gives an archeologically probable series of dates which also have a high mathematical probability of being correct. If accepted they demonstrate a system of recording which is intermediate between the Classic Initial Series and the Conquest period Katun Round.

The Maya calendar, although extremely accurate within itself, will be of complete service to us for tracing Maya history only after we know absolutely its correlation with our calendar. Our best direct material for such a correlation is a series of Conquest period references indicating that a Katun 13 Ahau ended between 1536 and 1541 A.D. The most circumstantial, and seemingly the most reliable, gives a day in 1539 A.D. Now we know that katuns ending in a 13 ahau occur on the Maya long count dates 10. 10. 0. 0. 0, 11. 3. 0. 0. 0, 11. 16. 0. 0. 0, 12. 9. 0. 0. 0 and every 13 katuns thereafter. 1539 A.D. must date later than 10. 3. 0. 0. 0, since we know that these carved dates preceded the Conquest; therefore one of the long count dates given above, or an even later Maya date, must equal 1539 A.D. From a variety of information derived from Maya historical chronicals written after the Conquest, from estimates derived from archeological cross-ties with the Mexican highland historical chronicles, and from certain astronomical data, it is generally conceded as very likely, although absolute certainty is at present impossible, that the Maya date 11. 16. 0. 0. 0 is equal to 1539 A.D. Less likely are 11. 3. 0. 0. 0 and 12. 9. 0. 0. 0, each of which is 13 katuns removed from the 11. 16. 0. 0. 0 correlation date. It is possible that the recently discovered radioactive carbon dating technique may eventually yield a positive decision between these possible correlations, but the margin of error of this technique within the pertinent dating range is so wide that the use of determinations from a considerable series of specimens will be necessary to attain reasonable certainty between the 256 year intervals.

Because of the present uncertainty in correlation, Maya dates are used in the description of the Classic stage in this text. The table which follows can be used for approximate conversion to the Christian calendar according to the 11. 16. 0. 0. 0 correlation.

8.14.0.0.0	317 A.D.	9.12.0.0.0	672 A.D.
8.16.0.0.0	357	9.14.0.0.0	711
8.18.0.0.0	396	9.16.0.0.0	751
9.0.0.0.0	435	9.18.0.0.0	790
9.2.0.0.0	475	10.0.0.0.0	830
9.4.0.0.0	514	10.2.0.0.0	869
9.6.0.0.0	554	10.4.0.0.0	909
9.8.0.0.0	593	10.6.0.0.0	948
9.10.0.0.0	633	10.9.0.0.0	987

The best text on the Maya calendar is S. G. Morley, *An Introduction to the Study of the Maya Hieroglyphs*, Bureau of American Ethnology, Bull. 57, Washington, 1915.

CERAMICS

Maya pottery at the height of its development is distinguished by the virtuosity characteristic of other Maya craft products, but the tradition of this craft shares much with the pottery of the rest of the New World. We know the pottery particularly well because of its usefulness in archeological dating.

Maya pottery was made of clay to which crushed mineral or pottery had been added. Although care in finishing the pottery usually makes it difficult to be certain of the technique of construction, forming seems to have been by hand coiling, perhaps aided by a device known as the *kabal*, followed by scraping. In some regions and time periods, vessels were occasionally formed by pressing clay into molds, and luting the molded pieces together. The potter's wheel was not used,

although a similar effect was obtained by other means,
Slip casting was never employed.

FORM REPERTORY

The kinds of pottery vessels used were quite constant over
the Maya area through a long time period, and most of the
major forms still survive and give us clues as to their original
use (fig. 13). Cooking jars, used for boiling over an open
fire, were a common and basic type. These have a round-
bottomed globular body with slightly constricted neck, and
short, flaring lip. They are not slipped, and those of the

FIG. 13—THE COMMON FORMS OF POTTERY VESSELS OF THE PUUC REGION,
YUCATAN, LATE CLASSIC STAGE. *a*, Cooking pot. *b*, Carrying and storage
jar. *f*, Jar used for drawing water from cisterns and for transport. *h*,
Basin. *i*, Incensario. *c-e*, *g*, *j*, Bowls of various sorts. *a*, *i*, Unslipped.
b, *d*, *f*, *h*, *j*, Medium slateware. *c*, Puuc Fine Orangeware, incised through
white slip. *e*, *g*, Thin slateware. *e* bears an underslip incised design. *a* is
18 inches high.

Maya area were usually raked with a rough tool to give the
exterior a striated surface which may have allowed more
efficient heat absorption. Walls are of an even thinness,
doubtless to minimize cracking under heat. Comales, low
flat trays of non-slipped pottery, were used for roasting
tortillas and other food. They are found in the highland Maya
area, the Motagua valley and elsewhere, but are rare or
lacking in the central and northern Maya area, suggesting
that the tortilla was little eaten there. In archeological times,
as now, corn was probably eaten as a gruel.

Water jars, used certainly in carrying and storing liquids,
and in some cases probably for drawing drinking water from
wells and cisterns, are slipped exteriorly, of markedly variable

size and form, usually with flattened bottom, and with necks higher and narrower than those of the cooking jars. They often bear handles for carrying and are of sizes appropriate to their varied uses.

Bowls are usually slipped internally, and over at least the upper part of the exterior. Volumes range from somewhat more than a pint to about two quarts, a size suggesting that they were used for serving food. Two forms, hemispheroid and flat-bottomed with low sloping sides are found. They nearly always have vessel supports, either a ring or three legs added to the bottom to afford stability to the vessel. Often the legs are hollow, enclosing pellets which rattle when the vessel is moved.

Basins and platters are usually considerably larger than are bowls. Form ranges from hemispheroid to a much shallower segment of a sphere. The bottom is most commonly flattened, but sometimes bears supports as do the bowls. The rim is usually thickened for strength. The interior, and often the exterior, is slipped. These basins were probably used in the preparation of cornmeal and gruels as are similar forms today. They may have held the day's allowance of corn for a family.

Fine ware vessels, thinner walled and often elaborately decorated, form a minor constituent of almost all Maya pottery collections. They were widely traded, but are small enough and often numerous enough to suggest that some of them were used even among the common people for serving individual portions of food. They are usually exteriorly slipped, often also have a slip interiorly. Common forms are beakers and tumblers, pyriform vessels on tall bases, cylinders, effigy forms.

Incensarios, still used for burning copal incense and for other religious uses among the modern Lacandone Maya, are not slipped, are usually decorated with appliqué, and covered with white unfired clay or plaster. Most of them are in the form of bowls or low cylinders supported on circular flaring bases, in late post Classic times a new anthropomorphic style was introduced. Incense ladles or dippers also appear in various Maya regions during Classic and post Classic times, presumably due to religious influence from the Mexican mainland.

DECORATIVE TECHNIQUES

The decorative techniques used for ceramics can, for convenience in description, be divided into techniques of surface coating and of surface alteration. In all but possibly

earliest Formative times all pottery save for cooking and ceremonial wares was painted with a surface coating or slip
of fine, often brightly colored, clay. With one localized exception, that of Plumbate pottery made in late Classic and
early post Classic times, Maya pottery was left unglazed.
Painting of pottery ranging up to four or five colors was
done at various times and places as was polished plaster or
gesso coating over slipped, previously fired fine ware. These
coatings were decorated by painting or by cloisonné-like
plaster inlay techniques. Unslipped ceremonial vessels were
customarily crudely painted after firing with lime or white clay
supplemented with other colors in a technique quite distinct
from, and cruder than, that of the polished plaster.

Widely varying techniques of surface alteration were employed, with varied effects. Of these, appliqué of hand-modeled
and mold-pressed elements should be mentioned, and hand-
modeling of the vessel surface. Also incision or engraving is
used, incision combined with carving to produce plano-relief,
stamping with tools ranging from a point to an elaborate
pottery stamp, burnishing, scraping with a rough tool, and
pressing parts of the vessel walls into clay molds. The appearance of work done by the above techniques was varied by the
degree of drying to which the clay was subjected before
decoration, and to the use of the surface alteration techniques
without slip, and before or after slipping or painting. Occasionally crude incising was done after the vessel was fired,
but likely not by the original potters.

There is archeological evidence of much variation through
time and between regions in the fashions of pottery decoration.
Evidence of invention and development is less certain than
was thought a few years ago, due to the recent finding of surprisingly advanced Formative pottery in the Guatemala highlands (fig. 3). Burnishing to produce surface patterns on unslipped pottery occurs in the earliest Formative horizons in both
Yucatan and Guatemala, and careful burnishing of slipped
surfaces seems commonest in Formative pottery. Both types
of post-firing coating were also in use by late Formative times.
Hand-modeled decoration seems to have been employed during
the whole time range, and incision and carving were likewise
universally used in many variants. Stamping and mold-pressing
do not seem to have become popular among the Maya until
late Classic times, although they began in early Classic times
on the Mexican mainland. The Formative stage flat and
cylindrical stamps of the Guatemala highlands were probably

used for the printing of textiles rather than for ceramic stamping. Painting with a second color on slip is known for the earliest Formative horizons in highland Guatemala; elsewhere it began to be used sparingly beginning in late Formative times. Polychrome, in two or more colors on a slip, is a Classic stage diagnostic in the Maya area, with the further restriction that black outlining of red or yellow areas was used on most examples, and that painted outlining seems to have replaced an earlier practice of outlining by an incised line.

TECHNIQUES OF MANUFACTURE

Several specialized ceramic techniques were used in the Maya area. In vessel-forming the use of the kabal is of particular

FIG. 14—YUCATAN POTTER USING A KABAL. He is scraping and expanding the pot with an oval gourd tool. Note carefully executed moldings on bowl to left. (Photograph by the author.)

interest (fig. 14). The kabal survives only in Yucatan at present, but simpler techniques which may be based on the same principles are found on the Mexican mainland and in the Guatemalan highlands. The pottery is coiled on a small cylinder of wood, the kabal, which rests on a smooth plank. The kabal is turned between the soles of the potter's feet during forming, and the vessel is coiled and shaped by the hands in a technique common to most areas where aboriginal pottery is made. During the final stages of the work, however, the vessel may be spun rapidly against the hands which guide the clay in almost precisely the manner used by modern potters in wheel-throwing. Modern vessels made by this technique have elaborate moldings and rims which appear wheel-turned, and such elaborations are common on Maya archeological pottery at least as far back as early Classic times, thus suggesting that the technique is an old one in the Maya area. The kabal in Yucatan has successfully competed with the wheel in the modern craft; in fact some workmen who are proficient in both prefer the kabal. With little question, this "wheel without an axle" represents a primitive mass production technique which gave an advantage of greater speed and precision, as well as greater latitude in vessel-forming to those who mastered it.

The forming of vessels by pressing clay into molds, then luting together the partially dried halves, is known from the Mexican and Maya highlands in early Classic times and has probably survived until now in highland Mexico; it also has a long history in Peru. The use of this advanced technique is undocumented as yet for the central Maya area and Yucatan and, although it may have been used there in prehispanic times, was probably never common or important.

Maya techniques of surface coating present several points of interest. The slips are nearly always applied by brushing rather than by dipping. Slips consist of fine white, cream, buff, orange, red, or brown clays, all of which show varying degrees of opacity and are applied in varying thickness, which thus permits a modification of the color by that of the underlying clay. The so-called slatewares of Yucatan were slipped with a clay which was translucent enough to have had little effect on the color of the underlying clay. Double coats of slip have been recognized on some varieties of Maya ceramics; an underslip of light-colored clay was covered with a somewhat translucent highly colored slip which thus gains brilliancy of color from the light background, giving the same effect as do "glazes" in oil painting. Such double slips are prone to flake off from Maya pottery. A coating of an organic stuff, a lacquer or something similar, is suspected to have been used for brilliancy and durability over some slips. The slips are all, of course, applied before firing, the organic coats presumably after. Two other post-firing surface-coating techniques are mentioned above, *gesso* (*yeso*) and white paint. Both of these are documented from Formative times on.

Two types of pre-firing paint are discernible: mineral and carbonaceous. The mineral paints have the same palette as do the slips, with the addition of brownish black. They consist of oxides of iron and manganese, probably applied in an aqueous solution containing organic substances. They were usually applied with a brush of some kind. Designs vary from broad-line geometric figures into naturalistic painting and glyphs done in styles so close to those of Maya codices as to suggest that the same artists may have worked in both media (fig. 15). The handsomest of the Maya polychrome vases are

FIG. 15—POLYCHROME VASE FROM CHAMA, GUATEMALA, SHOWING THE BAT GOD; LATE CLASSIC STAGE. Background is orange, scrolls and wing borders red, body brown, wings deep blue. Note Maya glyphs at right. Height of vase 7½ inches. (Drawing by the author after a watercolor by M. Louise Baker.)

unique in New World ceramics for virtuosity of painting. The finest of the naturalistic style seem localized in the northern foothills of the Guatemala highlands. The carbonaceous paints were applied as suspensions of organic, probably vegetal, substances in water. Firing, at the low temperatures used by the Maya and with the types of slips used, causes such paints to burn to carbon and leave the carbon embedded as a dark, often mottled stain within the lighter colored slip. Under smoky firing conditions the slip often turns a darker color, and the painted areas a lighter tone. This color reversal sometimes occurs only on parts of the vessel. Carbonaceous paint was usually applied in heavy lines or blobs, and the paint seems often to have been gelatinous when used. Yucatan slateware was normally decorated with carbonaceous paint.

The firing of Maya pottery was done at low temperature. No sure evidence of precolumbian kilns has been found, although kilns are in use now in the area. Kilns would not have been technically essential to produce the range of ceramics known. Whatever the equipment, there is evidence that good control of firing temperature and of atmospheric conditions during firing were well within Maya capabilities.

GRAPHIC ART

Maya graphic art, like most of the great art styles of the world, is characterized by an over-all unity, easily definable by the recognition of a group of conventions or formalities, ways of representing objects, of drawing designs, to which its products were restricted. Conventions of the arts of foreign peoples invariably seem bizarre on first sight. Their strangeness is likely to dominate our attention to the detriment of esthetic enjoyment, and our judgment of quality is often blinded by unfamiliarity, or at best limited to the qualities, such as those dependent on realism and geometric relations, which may be judged regardless of the cultural background of the viewer.

Maya artistic conventions can be divided into two groups on the basis of hypothesized function: (a) decorative, (b) symbolic. Most of Maya art is founded ultimately in actual objects: it can be called in the main a representational art, but its realism can be appreciated only after the often complex conventions used can be resolved in some degree by the viewer. The effectiveness of its purely decorative elements depends on factors of balance, symmetry, and proportion which, although often complex to grasp, may be considered universal in their appeal.

The symbolic meanings of Maya art, although they obviously bore strong emotional appeal to the ancient Maya, are in great part permanently lost. A religious art is impossible to grasp emotionally without a thorough grounding in the religion; how much European Renaissance religious art would be comprehensible to one who did not know of Christianity? The pervasive, molding effects of the religion of the Maya on their arts has been well put by Spinden:

> . . . religion, as a communal element in the life of the nation, turns the attention of all artists to a common purpose. Through this focusing of the attention, religion leads inevitably to an intensive rather than a diffuse development of art. But once this intensive development has exhausted the possibilities of the established ideas, then religion throws its powerful influence against further disorganizing change. Thus religion enriches art and makes it permanent.

The realistic content of Maya art, particularly bas relief sculpture, is made more difficult of appreciation to most of us by the very involved and closely spaced composition characteristic of much of it. Accustomed as we are to emphasis by the use of plain backgrounds, the tightly composed panels of the Maya at first sight appear cluttered. Closer inspection and an effort at analysis is necessary to reveal the subtle emphasis of lines and planes which in the best of it were used to disengage the points of interest from the surrounding detail. This preliminary task of attention is doubtless heightened in difficulty by the fact that most Maya sculptures were planned for painting in colors. Such painting, of course, aided the eye in its analysis of the composition.

Maya graphic art is known in three major techniques: *painting* on plaster walls, pottery, and sized paper; *carving* on wood, shell, bone, soft stone (architectural and monumental sculpture), and hard stone (lapidary carving); *modeling* in clay and stucco. Metallurgy was unknown here in the Classic stage. Among minor art techniques, plaster inlay, and mosaic work in shell and stone should be mentioned, and elaborate weaving and embroidery of designs in cotton cloth may safely be hypothesized from its representation on costumed Maya personages.

SCULPTURE

Maya sculpture with its closely related architecture (see pages 26-39) is the most famous of the Maya arts. The sculpture was all done with stone tools. In most of the Maya area limestone was used exclusively, although in some regions sandstone and volcanic rock were the materials. The technique was in the main pecking with a hard stone tool, often supplemented by a final smoothing by grinding with an abrasive stone or powder.

The objects carved are in the main free standing stelæ and altars, and objects used for architectural embellishment. Stelæ are vertically set, free standing monuments made from single large stone slabs, the largest of which, Stela E at Quirigua, is 35 feet long with an estimated weight of 65 tons. Style of carving on stelæ ranges from simple incised outlining, through intaglio refinements of the same, plano-relief with incised detail on the raised surfaces, finely graduated relief, running from low to full, into sculpture which, although it approaches completely rounded, naturalistic representation, usually shows a clinging to the original, usually squarish form of the stone block, and a tendency toward the incising of surface detail. The stela as an art form is assumed by Maya students to have originated in the central or Classic Maya area where it was used for the inscription of Initial Series dates, although its occasional presence and use for dates and inscriptions in highland Guatemala and in the Olmec, Zapotec, and Totonac areas makes its origin elsewhere possible. The art of stela carving diffused to some degree into Yucatan where, however, stelæ often do not bear Initial Series dates, but it outlived the Initial Series period only slightly, if at all. Altars normally accompany stelæ in the Maya area, but often are not carved. The huge and elaborate animal-formed altars of Quirigua are the outstanding examples of this form.

The subject matter of the stela carving is remarkably uniform in all areas and over the 550 year span documented by the carved dates. Nearly all stelæ of the central Maya area are decorated with a single, elaborately costumed male figure carved in bas-relief. This figure, either priest, ruler, or god, dominates the composition and his tremendous plume-bedecked headdress is often fitted closely to a border which frames the front face of the stela. Rectangular or L-shape panels of glyphs included in the front panel give dates or, presumably, descriptive material, and additional human figures, usually smaller than the main figure, appearing to be acolytes, slaves,

or captives, are frequently shown. Additional decorative and
glyphic panels often were carved on the sides and, less often,
on the back of the stela. Stelæ were most frequently set on
a low platform in a plaza at the foot of the central staircase
ascending to a major temple. Additional stelæ were added
after the first, normally forming a row or cluster, at the ends
of successive 20-year or even 5- or 10-year calendric periods.

The close dating given by the chronological inscriptions on
some 400 known Maya sculptured monuments has attracted
various students to studies of the development through time

Fig. 16—CARVING ON ALTAR 2. BONAMPAK, CHIAPAS. Proskouriakoff dates
this altar c. 700 A.D., in her Formative phase of the Late Classic period.
Note the use of delicately modulated incised lines and a minimum of intaglio
surface modeling. (Photograph courtesy of Giles G. Healey.)

of this art. The most recent study of this sort, by Proskouriakoff, points up the intensely conservative tradition of Maya
sculpture: the composition of the bas-reliefs, even the costuming and accessories of the figures, shows remarkably
little change over 550 years. The changes observable are
mainly in style of representation rather than in subject
matter. Miss Proskouriakoff differentiates a first phase of ex-
perimentation and diversity (8.14.0.0.0 - 9.0.0.0.0). Her
Early Period (8.14.0.0.0 - 9.5.0.0.0) as a whole shows a
preoccupation with the symbolic subject matter at the expense

of naturalism. The objects depicted are shown in the position and from the viewpoint which best exhibits their specific attributes, but often departs radically from realistic representation. There is a thus far unexplained break in the continuity of stela erection for some 60 years between 9.5.0.0.0 and 9.8.0.0.0.

In the Late Classic period (9.8.0.0.0 - 10.3.0.0.0) there is a growing emphasis on realism, although the symbolism is of course still retained. The Formative phase (9.8.0.0.0 - 9.13.0.0.0) shows the emergence of the regional late Classic styles (see fig. 16). The Ornate phase of the late Classic period (9.13.0.0.0 - 9.16.0.0.0) shows the beginnings of a

Fig. 17—DETAIL OF STELA 1, BONAMPAK, CHIAPAS. This stela is placed by Proskouriakoff in her Dynamic phase and dated *c.* 770-850 A.D. (Photograph courtesy of Giles G. Healey.)

"progressive elaboration of artificial rhythmic modulations in line and relief superimposed on the conception of objects as mere physical entities." This rhythmic stylization adds a feeling of tension, a dynamic quality, to the composition. The dynamic quality described by Proskouriakoff for this sculpture should not be misunderstood to mean the use of compositions showing movement in the human figures, but is caused rather by a rhythmic composition in the details of the figure and costuming. It is during the sequent Dynamic phase (9.16.0.0.0 - 9.19.0.0.0) that Maya sculpture reached its highest development (see fig. 17). As suggested above,

the close spaced elaboration which characterizes much
sculpture of this period is saved from chaos by a remarkably
developed sense of composition and balance: "order in complexity" as Proskouriakoff puts it.

The Phase of Decadence (9.19.0.0.0 - 10.3.0.0.0) shows a
marked breakaway from the realism of the earlier phases; it
is sacrificed to a greater interest to two-dimensional pattern,
a pattern achieved by a simplification of the earlier delicately
modeled bas relief into plano-relief carving. There is a de-
gradation in form and distortion in scale of objects to suit a
new set of conventions which, although their connotative
effect on the symbolically conditioned Maya is hard to gauge,
is difficult for the modern viewer to appreciate.

The regional variations in Classic Maya sculpture are also
considerable, even though the sculptures of the Initial Series
stelæ are in Proskouriakoff's judgment distinguished by a
remarkable coherence and absence of outside influence. In
discussing the regional variants of the Classic Maya area
sculpture during the Initial Series period, the constancy of
design through time on stelæ from single sites should be
stressed; this would be expected if a single group or school
of sculptors developed, with examples of their earlier work
constantly before them. Examples of deliberate archaism noted
on late sculptures may logically be laid to this same tendency
to copy locally visible early carvings. The developmental
style sequences differ somewhat in detail but are similar in
general trends for the various Peten sites during the Initial
Series period.

In regions other than the Central Maya area there were
striking and obvious regional variants such as the western
development of superlative naturalistic relief and intaglio
styles, the Copan development of sculpture in the round,
and a variety of styles in Yucatan which Proskouriakoff
believes show many archaic as well as foreign features. Still
farther afield, the area of the Isthmus of Tehuantepec and
adjoining coastal areas, including the so-called Totonac and
Zapotec regions of the southeastern Mexican mainland, show
highly developed local styles which can be related to the Classic
Maya only in a more general manner.

Maya woodcarving is known chiefly from zapote wood
lintels, the finest specimens of which come from the temple
doorways at Tikal. The technique is low relief, the style and
subject matter close to that of the stonecarving. It has been
assumed by some that wooden stelæ were carved in a period

preceding that of the earliest stone stelæ, but no archeological evidence of such carving has ever been found. We have documentary accounts of many wooden "idols" at Conquest times, but unfortunately none of these has survived.

MURALS

Maya mural painting of the Classic stage is known from the superb examples at Bonampak, Chiapas (see fig. 18), and from much less elaborate and less well preserved examples from Uaxactun, and from the Puuc and Chenes areas. All these murals show scenes centering about groups of human figures in costume. They are narrative in character. The technique at Bonampak, according to Agustín Villagra, was *fresco,* with a palette of ten mineral colors. The drawing was first cartooned with a pale-red line, the enclosed areas painted in, after which black outlining was added. Villagra detects no jointing between the areas of fresh plaster, and therefore assumes that a considerable number of men did the plaster laying and painting as a continuous process. As in all other known Precolumbian art, no intentional shading to show surface modeling was used, but much skill in the use of color contrast is evident and several tones of the same color, apparently produced by overpainting, were achieved. The scenes show lively action and considerable intentional variation in facial expression and in body build. The conventions in figure drawing are those of the contemporary bas-relief sculpture of this region; bodies are shown in profile, full face, or twisted with almost unlimited freedom of posture. Faces, however, are always turned in profile. Depth is attained in the pictures by superposition of objects and, in some of the murals, by the choice of pyramid steps as a setting. The figures on these steps are naturally thrown into several horizontal bands or registers, the lower figures superimposed against the upper. No linear perspective or diminution of size with distance was used. The linework is exquisitely done, curved outlines are handled with virtuosity. The scenes from the three Bonampak rooms show ceremonies and sacrifices, the robing of priests and, surprisingly for the Classic Maya for whom we have little evidence of warfare, a battle scene. The information given on Maya costuming, as well as on Maya life by these elaborate scenes is great, but has not at this writing been summarized in published form. The presence of descriptive glyph panels as well as calendric dates in cursive script suggests that the artists were members of the educated religious hierarchy.

Painted scenes bearing a close similarity to the murals are found on polychrome pottery, the manufacture of which centered in the northern foothills of the Guatemalan highlands during the latter half of the Classic period. These scenes are of course smaller and more simple than the murals, and the included glyph panels are crudely done, suggesting that the artisans did not usually understand the hieroglyphic script. In the early half of the Classic stage the designs painted on pottery are in main part abstract, but show a gradual increase

Fig. 18—SACRIFICIAL VICTIM. DETAIL OF A FRESCO WALL DECORATION FROM ROOM 2 AT BONAMPAK, CHIAPAS. (Infra red photograph courtesy of Giles G. Healey.)

of interest in naturalistic representation and in the ornamental use of glyphs. From the following Toltec period at Chichen Itza, Yucatan, a considerable number of elaborate murals are known. These are, however, drawn in the foreign Mexican mainland style, although probably by Maya craftsmen.

There are three known Maya manuscripts, or codices, which date from just before or somewhat after the close of the Classic stage. They are long, accordion-folded sheets of bark paper, the surfaces of which have been sized with a white plaster-like coat. The bulk of the drawing on the codices is of hieroglyphs; the picture panels which are included are simpler and more stylized than the naturalistic mural and pottery designs. The rounded, cursive glyphs used in these codices must have evolved during use on painted manuscripts, but these forms were occasionally copied in stone sculpture as well (see fig. 16), although most sculptured glyphs are of squarish, formal type.

MODELING

The beginnings of the art of modeling in the Maya area stretch back to the Formative stage, and both stucco and clay were used this early. The massive, markedly conventionalized masks of temple E-VII sub, Uaxactun, (fig. 4) set the symbolic, religiously oriented style from which later developments diverge, mainly in the direction of greater intricacy, and, in some periods and areas, into greater naturalism. The development of stucco work rather closely parallels that in stone, and at various sites, notably Palenque, they seem to have been used nearly interchangeably. The prevalence of stucco ornamentation applied in heavy mass to crude stone surfaces with projecting tenons on early Classic buildings suggests that Maya stone-carving may owe important elements of its style to stucco-modeling, particularly the characteristic smooth flowing linework which is so much easier to attain in that technique. It should be remembered that nearly all Maya stone-carving was finished with a layer of stucco whereby the rough surface angles of the worked stone could be smoothed and the lines of the composition given the sweep and curve characteristic of good stucco-modeling.

It is unfortunate that stucco has lasted so•poorly. A few fragmentary stucco-decorated façade zones and roof combs suggest that elaborate ceremonial scenes were depicted in bas relief on long panels, somewhat as were the scenes of the Bonampak murals. The ease in designing large surfaces may have encouraged larger naturalistic compositions; some of these may yet be found.

Terracotta was little used for architectural ornament, although there is an area near Comalcalco where fired bricks replace stone in construction. But clay figurines at their finest reinforce the Maya claim of New World preëminence in naturalistic art. Effigy vessels are known from the early Classic stage, but are neither common nor highly d e v e l o p e d. The greatest concen- tration, as well as the greatest height of figurine develop- ment is found in the burial offerings in cemeteries on the Island of Jaina, off the north Cam- peche coast (see fig. 19). Related figurines are found, though less f r e - quently, throu g h - out the Campeche and Tabasco low- lands, and generally similar types occur in Veracruz. They are usually made of a fine-textured, orange burning clay; they are

Fig. 19—Hand-modeled figurine from the Island of Jaina, Campeche. Height 7½ inches.

either hand-modeled or mold-pressed. Ruz believes that the hand-modeled type was made at about 9.10.0.0.0, and this date seems plausible. Mold-pressed figurines seem generally charac- teristic of the Late Classic stage in the north and central Maya areas.

The scale of these figurines is miniature, seldom much more than six inches in height, and the detail is finer than in any other New World ceramics. The hand-modeled figurines are constructed completely in the round and are chiefly men. They normally have no base, and most often are of solid clay. Faces are less than an inch long, exquisitely modeled, in some cases showing tattooing. Clothing, including elaborate head- dresses, is added in appliqué. Figures are standing or seated naturalistically, musculature is sparingly shown. The mold-pressed figurines are made of two thin slabs of clay, joined around their edges. The front of the figurine has been pressed into a clay mold, and such molds have been found. Pellets are often inserted before adding the plain back to make a rattle with one or two small perforations. In other figurines a whistle is modeled in at an inconspicuous place along the edge or on the back to form a two- or three-stopped ocarina. The mold-front figurines most often show women in huipiles; also animals, an animal with a human, or a couple, man and woman, are shown. Both seated and standing postures are used, and quite often details are sharpened with hand-tooling and added by appliqué. A few figurines have been found together in such manner as to suggest that they were used to arrange a simple tableau, but most seem to have been designed singly.

Spinden, H. J., *A Study of Maya Art*, Cambridge, 1913, gives the best discussion of Maya art. Kelemen, Pal., *Medieval American Art*, New York, 1943, and Morley, S. G., *The Ancient Maya*, Stanford, 1946, contain the best series of illustrations. Proskouriakoff, Tatiana, *A Study of Classic Maya Sculpture*, Washington, 1950, is the best in its field.

DRESS

In the warm climate of the Maya area, clothing as protection from the elements has never been a necessity. Maya clothing was esteemed as decoration, and its most spectacular examples were worn by the priests. Seldom in the world have such magnificent costumes been seen.

The Classic Maya had no metals, and their jewelry was therefore restricted to cut stone. This was often combined with the brilliant feathers of tropical birds to make the tremendous and fantastic headdresses worn by Maya personages (fig. 20). Large ear-plugs, necklaces, breast-plates, ornaments attached to the nose, lips, waist, legs, arms, all were used with involved and resplendent effect. Added to the impact of this magnificence on the Maya commoners was the religious awe which the priests, dressed to represent the gods, must have evoked. Intricate weavings and embroideries were also worn. Large parasols and decorated litters were used as accouterments, as were delicately decorated circular mirrors with a reflecting surface of polished iron pyrite, cemented in mosaic fashion onto one face. Scepters were carried by these dignitaries, before whom groveled fettered captives. Rulers sat cross-legged on platform-like thrones which were often covered with jaguar-skins; they are shown on occasion surrounded by servants as

FIG. 20—THE ROBING OF A MAYA PRIEST. BONAMPAK, CHIAPAS, TEMPLE OF
THE MURALS, ROOM 1, detail. (Redrawn from a watercolor by Villagra)

well as by lesser officials. With no question the ceremonies were confined to, or at least led by, the men; there are few women shown in Maya religious art, and they were subordinate in social position at the time of the Conquest.

Information on the costuming of the common man is harder to obtain. Maya art, our main source, was strongly oriented toward religion and its panoply. The costuming shown on some of the pottery figurines is simpler, but nevertheless the ever-present headdress is too bulky to have been worn by the common man during his labors. The essential items, shown in all representations, were loin-cloths and strapped sandals. Women are more often shown in figurines than in other art. Commonly shown on figurines of women was the *huipil*, a sack-like garment with neck-hole woven in, and arm-holes left unsewn in the side borders. This garment was often worn over a skirt which was gathered and tied around the waist, and which in some areas was worn without the huipil. A cloak, which seems to have been a square or rectangle of cloth or an animal skin, was used by both men and women to cover the upper part of the body. Cloaks used for ceremonial wear were often covered with exceedingly handsome featherwork. The hair of both men and women was elaborately dressed, as part of the headgear. The men burned off tonsures on top of the head.

The modern Maya men invariably wear broad-brimmed straw hats (fig. 21). Hats with brim and crown occasionally appear on figurines and sculpture, but their material cannot be recognized. The *sabucan*, a rectangular henequen bag, is always borne by the Maya countryman, who carries his goods, tools, and personal supplies in it. Such bags are common in pre-Conquest Peru and over modern Mexico. I know of no archeological evidence for the use of the *sabucan* in the Maya area, and the absence of a Maya name for the object suggests that their use is post-Conquest only. A gourd canteen with a corn-cob plug and a constricted band about its middle is also a part of the Yucatan male costume when traveling or working. The canteen is likely pre-Conquest, since we know from Landa's account that native gourds were commonly used for vessels when the Spaniards arrived. The modern Maya farmer seldom moves without his machete, which he uses for cutting paths and *milpa,* and even for eating and cosmetic purposes. It is difficult to imagine how he worked without one! A rifle or shotgun is often carried, and blowguns are occasionally seen in the Guatemala highlands. The commonest Classic Maya weapon was a long lance, often elaborately decorated with feathers. Flint- or obsidian-edged swords, hafted stone celts, and clubs or maces are also seen in Classic Maya sculpture. Rectangular shields were carried. Long wooden trumpets were used in warfare. In ceremonies, trumpets, pottery drums with skin heads, and a wide variety of turtleshell and gourd rattles gave music.

FIG. 21—A YUCATECAN FARMER RETURNING FROM HIS FIELD. The steel *coa* is used mainly for weeding. (Photo by W. D. Chester)

SETTLEMENT PATTERN

Our archeological knowledge of the living arrangements of the Maya of the Classic period is of necessity largely inferential. The Maya-speaking peoples in both the Highland and Yucatan areas at the time of the Spanish Conquest were found living in towns from which they walked to their cornfields. But descriptions from Conquest and modern sources must be treated with reserve, since we know that the Maya had without question been subjected to strong influence from the Mexican mainland beginning before 1000 A.D.

There are several lines of evidence, no one conclusive but all highly suggestive, that the Classic Maya lived in small settlements or in single houses evenly spread over the country, and that they gathered in their ceremonial centers only at times of religious festival. As has been remarked earlier, there is some evidence of Formative village settlements in at least some parts of the Maya area. The Lacandones, the modern Maya group least affected by European culture, make pilgrimages to Classic Maya sites to leave offerings. This practice is still observed to some extent over most of the Maya area, and is documented archeologically as well by finds of late incense burners in early temples. In the Guatemala Highlands the Maya towns are fully inhabited only at times of marketing and religious holidays; the Indians live on their land for the rest of the year. This pattern is also found, but to a lesser degree, in modern Yucatan.

At the Classic site of Uaxactun a survey for house ruins was made over a cross-shaped area just under four square miles in extent, centering at the religious site. Fifty-two housemounds were found quite evenly distributed over all land suitable for building, suggesting that such an even house-patterning may have covered much or all of the lowland Maya area during the Classic stage. This pattern is strikingly different from that at the Mexican period Yucatecan site of Mayapan, where a recent survey shows that an estimated 3500 houses were concentrated within a walled area of only 1.6 square mile. The striking contrast of 69 houses per square mile as compared with about 220 per square mile is heightened by the likelihood that at Uaxactun, which was used for nearly a thousand years, only a portion of the houses surveyed were inhabited simultaneously. At Mayapan, a short period site, the greater part of the houses must have been occupied at once.

From Yucatan there is both linguistic and archeological evidence that the concept of the town as a concentrated human settlement, as well as the concept of warfare, has Mexican origins, introduced in the main during Toltec or somewhat later times. It has generally been assumed that the prominence of militarism in late times must have caused a shift from priestly to secular authority. There is more than a hint from Yucatan archeology that the centers of population at the time of the Toltec influx shifted from the Puuc hill region to the northern plain. This was likely the result of Toltec attempts at easier administration and government. Finally, there is reason to suspect from the marked diversity of Classic stage culture among Yucatan, the Peten, and the Guatemala highlands that social organization and settlement pattern may have varied among the subdivisions of the Maya area.

The soil and climate of the lowland Maya area must have limited the type of agriculture practicable there to some system not far from the slash-burn agriculture now practiced in Yucatan. Under slash-burn agriculture, rotation of land is at present a necessity. One crop a year is raised in most of Yucatan, although as many as three are reported from wetter areas. Not more than a sixth of the land is under cultivation at one time. This situation stands in marked contrast to that of semi-arid highland areas and river valleys, where irrigation and fertilization of soil may have allowed continued argiculture in certain areas favored by a dependable water supply, and thus have fostered the growth of concentrated human settlements.

As has been pointed out earlier, the development of an elaborate civilization by a thinly spread human group does not conform to the currently accepted reconstruction of history in other Old and New World areas. The Maya had the leisure for nonutilitarian pursuits, but it is hard to see how they could have been subjected to the economic compulsion which can easily be exercised by the rulers of an irrigated area. It would seem that the Maya may have furnished their own goad to advancement, if a goad can be assumed always to be needed, in the form of an all-absorbing religion.

SOCIAL ORGANIZATION

Our evidence for Classic Maya social structure is of necessity more inferential and thus more precarious than that for settlement pattern. The overlay of Mexican mainland culture is evident in the Maya chronicles of the Conquest period. In these, the Yucatecan and Guatemalan political rulers have Nahua names and boast of Mexican origins, although those of Yucatan

seem to have come from Tabasco. It is unmistakable in the
representational art of Toltec Chichen Itza, where Mexican
military insignia dominate the scene. Political rulers and military men indubitably followed Mexican prototypes, both in
Toltec and Conquest times. There is also evidence for worship
of Kukulcan, the feathered serpent god (Mexican Quetzalcoatl), for the practice of human sacrifice in the Mexican manner, for the use of racks for the skulls of sacrificial victims,
and for numerous other Mexican copyings. There are suggestions, however, that the veneer of Toltec religion was at least
partially sloughed off in subsequent times, and that Maya gods
and religious centers, Maya calendrics and writing, still retained their hold on the populace at the Conquest. In fact,
even now they play an important part in the lives of Maya
farmers.

So much for the evidence of Mexican origin of political,
religious, and military leadership in Yucatan. The people who
made these innovations are described in the chronicles as migra-
tory, and as having attained power through wisdom and gen-
erosity rather than by conquest, a characterization at variance
with their warlike accouterments in bas-reliefs and paintings
at Chichen Itza. Without doubt they constituted a sharply
marked, nonmobile caste in Yucatan until the Spanish Conquest; even their culture may have become largely Maya and
their blood have become mixed as well.

The war-chief (*halach uinic*) was the supreme military-
political commander of a province, the largest unit in Yucatan
at the time of the Conquest. The office was inherited patri-
lineally within a single family. The early Spanish described
the judicial and religious powers held by the halach uinic—he
was a bishop and a judge. His living was provided by tribute
levies and court fees, and he was given military aid by all
towns under his control. He possessed a considerable retinue,
and traveled by litter. The town-chief, or *batab,* was appoint-
ed by the halach uinic, but usually in hereditary succession
if the heir were considered suitable. Like the halach uinic, the
batab exercised administrative, judiciary, and miltary functions; he ruled over a town council and a whole hierarchy of
local officials. During warfare the batab shared his command
with a war-chief, the *nacom,* who held office for a three-year
term and led a ceremonially regulated life; he was supported
by a group of warriors, the *holcans,* professionals paid during
the war by the nacon and the town. All of these officials
are described by the early Spanish as also assuming religious

functions on occasion. Wars could be waged because of personal injuries done by foreigners, and such cases were brought before the nacom. The obtaining of slaves was another purpose of war. Wars were usually seasonal and were conducted during slack periods in agricultural activity. There is evidence for coastal raids on Yucatan by foreigners. The techniques of warfare have much in common with those of mainland Mexico, and can be assumed in great part, to stem from there, developed chiefly in post-Classic times.

The Maya, other than the "nobility" who boasted Mexican descent, were "commoners" who could be graded according to their wealth and by the proximity of their houses to the ceremonial area of the town. They could occupy minor political posts. Slaves, who often were used for sacrifice, were thieves, orphans, or captives. They were not held to their station by birth, but could gain their freedom.

The degree of similarity between Maya social structure at the time of the Conquest and that of the Classic Maya is problematic. The Mexican ruling caste of Yucatan may well have incorporated Maya attitudes toward authority in their rule of the conquered, thus producing a fusion of both systems only imperfectly analyzable by extraction of known Mexican customs. A few clues to Maya holdovers may be given. Landa, a sixteenth-century Bishop of Yucatan who is our best single source on the Conquest-period Maya, mentions a hereditary "high priest," who, although he had no retinue, received gifts from the people, was much respected by the lords, and was the authority on writing and calendrics, divination, healing, and antiquities. This individual, with his superior learning and a suggestion of aloofness from the hurlyburly of government, may conceivably have held the remnant of authority of the Maya ruler-priests. It is also known that the rulers of Yucatan had gods whom the common man was not permitted to worship. These gods were with little doubt Mexican importations, the chief among whom was Quetzalcoatl. This deity was never integrated into the Yucatecan pantheon, certain members of which are still worshipped by the Maya.

Our best view of life among the Maya elite of the Classic stage comes from the Bonampak murals, which show narrative scenes of ceremony, human sacrifice, and warfare. The personal interaction shown by the attitudes and expressions of the figurines provides unique data for an analysis of Maya social organization. Although the impressions recorded here are strengthened by harmonizing information from other sources, they must of course be taken as tentative. First, there is evidence that authority or status among the priests, as shown by elaboration of costume, was not concentrated in one individual. The high priest at the ceremony is flanked by eight others no less resplendent than himself, and the leaders in the battle are followed by others in equally magnificent headgear. Although it might be expected that commoners would not appear in the ceremonial groups, this should not be true in war, but there are certainly more generals than privates in the battle scene! In the ceremonial scenes there are several groupings which consist of two facing contingents of men, all robed in equal splendor. This suggests some sort of discussion between two delegations, each member of which held equal authority. Most of the people stand or sit in comfortable and highly individualistic poses, and many are in animated conversation; gesticulation, remarks made over the shoulder, are common. There is here no suggestion of regimentation or autocracy.

Although it seems clear that supreme authority was not vested in one person, there is much evidence of hierarchy of rank. The more elaborately costumed individuals are often flanked by plump attendants, several of whom are performing valet service for the magnificently robed priests. These men wear simpler headdresses than those of the chief dignitaries, and they wear neither mantles nor kilts. There is not the slightest formality nor servility in their bearing; they are shown gossiping with one another and with the functionaries. The only exception to this democratic impression is given by the fierce scowl of one priest who is having a bracelet adjusted by an attendant (fig. 20). Most of the musicians and parasol bearers wear elaborate kilts and headdresses. Jaguar-skins are worn by these men as well as by the more elaborately dressed functionaries. Glyph blocks which may bear names always adjoin the principal figures, but are not present near some of the more simply dressed individuals. The victims in the sacrifice scene may be distinguished from all other people by their absence of headgear, by the scanty simplicity of their loin-cloths, and by their braided hair. That they are captives is suggested by the neighboring murals which show the taking of prisoners as a part of the battle scene. These captives, minus their headgear and weapons, are being manhandled. The sacrifices are in charge of armed warriors of much more severe face and posture than those shown elsewhere in the ceremonies.

A few women and children are shown. Two women appear in commanding positions observing the sacrifices. They wear white huipiles and underskirts. In the ceremonial scene five women and a child in arms, all wearing white huipiles, are shown on and around a raised throne. In the robing scene a woman is shown on a throne, a small girl next to it, and a baby in arms nearby. The thrones, in the form of tables used as seats, are placed on pyramid tops in a position to view the proceedings. There is a suggestion here of a sort of "royal family," separate from the members of the priestly establishment who are performing the religious ceremony.

In interpreting these scenes it is well to remember the wide differences between the Maya cultural background and ours; we hold more culture in common with the Mesopotamia of 3000 B.C. than with the Maya shown here. Interpretations have necessarily been made in the above descriptions. We must also remember that the Bonampak murals are late Classic western Maya, and probably show more Mexican mainland influence than the majority of Classic Maya remains. They do suggest, however, that the concepts of a nobility, of some distinction between religious and secular authority and of captive slaves used for sacrifice, were a part of the Maya pattern of their time and place. The impression is also given of considerable camaraderie, at least among the favored group who dominate these paintings. The Bonampak murals seem to bear out inferences drawn from the Maya economy and settlement pattern, that repressive authority was not characteristic of the Classic Maya.

ECONOMY AND POPULATION

It has been estimated that from 75 to 85 percent of the diet of the Modern Maya consists of corn. Corn is intimately woven into the Maya religious symbolism of the Classic period, and in all likelihood was the staple food of the Maya area from early in the times of plant domestication. Since corn is almost exclusively a starch food, protein and mineral constituents must always have been supplied from other sources, which now include the meat of domesticated animals. In pre-Columbian times these sources must have consisted mainly of beans, supplemented by other plant foods, by such meat as could be obtained by hunting, and probably by the tame ducks described by early Spaniards. It may be added that the milpa agricultural system, which leaves most of the land in bush at all times, must have permitted the Maya more wild game than is available to most agriculturists. Salt and fish were obtained from the coastal areas and traded extensively inland.

Milpa or slash-burn agriculture is practiced by the lowland Maya by first clearing the heavy, usually thorny growth and allowing it to dry during the six-month dry season. Just before the rains begin in May or June, the cleared fields are burned over to destroy the felled timber, brush, and plant seeds. The corn is planted by means of a planting stick, in clusters which are often situated in crevasses in the ubiquitous limestone. Weeding is done once or more during the growth of the corn in the rainy season, in modern times rather haphazardly by cutting off the weeds with a machete. The various kinds of corn used ripen in from two to six months. When ripe, the tops of the corn-plants are bent over to protect the ears from rain and birds, and the corn is either picked for storage in cribs or caves or left in the field to pick for use as needed. Fields are usually sown two years in succession, the yield dropping off about a quarter the second year, due partially to the throttling effect of weeds. After a second crop the field is generally left for an average of ten years, until plant succession has given a growth high and dense enough to allow burning.

This system allows only about a fifth of the land to be cultivated at any one time. The limiting factor to more frequent use recognized by the modern Maya is the lack of sufficient vegetation to allow the burning over of land left for a shorter time. The only other method usable in clearing is hand-weeding. Although too laborious to be economically desirable at present, this would have had the advantage of not destroying, as does the burning, most of the organic constituents of the soil. Plowing, harrowing, cultivating, and other mechanized methods of land-clearing are impossible in most parts of Yucatan because of the extremely shallow and rocky soil.

The dry season of six months, coupled with the absence of streams for irrigation, further limits agricultural production. It has been suggested that were repeated cultivation possible, the land, constantly leached by tropical rains, would be rapidly depleted of nourishment and need frequent fallowing. However, in a plot of land in Yucatan which was experimentally irrigated, multiple-cropped and weeded for some twelve years, Steggerda, as reported by Morley, found that there was an initial drop in crop yield following the first year and that encroaching grass became increasingly difficult to handle, but that there was little or no depletion of the organic nitrogen in the soil. These results, although incomplete and debatable, suggest the possibility that competing vegetation, rather than diminishing soil fertility, may be the limiting factor for continued agricultural land use.

In the reconstruction of pre-Conquest Maya agriculture, the European addition which is hardest to imagine eliminated is the machete, which has become the principal tool of the Maya farmer. Without the steel machete, the labor of clearing and weeding was unquestionably much greater and the result attained must have been different than now in several respects. With stone tools, it must have been easiest to girdle the large trees a year early and then burn them in place; felling a tree with a stone axe would have been unnecessarily difficult. Small-sized tree-trunks and shrubs were probably cut and smaller plants could most easily have been pulled out by the roots, a more permanent although more laborious method than cutting with the machete. Landa mentions burning, and evidence from elsewhere in the New World suggests that this custom was widespread and must have preceded the Conquest in Yucatan.

From the above information it seems likely that the pre-Conquest Maya corn farmer tilled a smaller area and tilled it more intensively than now. With hand-weeding it may have been possible to clear the land at shorter intervals and desirable to raise several crops in succession. The time consumed in hand-weeding cannot have been an insurmountable handicap, since it has been calculated that the Modern Yucatecan farmer spends only about fifty days per year in raising enough corn for his family to eat. The advantage in hand-weeding may well have been the ability to keep weeds from strangling the crops during several successive years of cultivation on a single plot. The limit to the number of years during which a single plot could have been cultivated may have been set in part by the encroachment of sod, which must have been nearly impossible for the Maya to eradicate. In fact, it has been suggested that the fingerlike savannah areas in the Peten and other regions are possibly relics of grass-grown land which originally could have been a major cause of the Maya abandonment of agricultural areas.

From the figures given by Steggerda on agriculture among the Yucatan Maya, some estimates of Classic-stage Maya population may be attempted. The margin of error is bound to be great, but since the two most recent computations on population differ tremendously (Morley, 1946, estimates between 13,300,000 and 53,300,000; Termer, 1951, gives a total of 800,000; both these figures are for the whole lowland Maya area) it should pay to try estimates on separate data.

From Steggerda's figures it appears that 20 acres of ground will permanently supply enough corn to feed a family of five persons in modern Yucatan. If 100,000 square miles be taken as the approximate area of the Lowland Maya culture area, a maximum population of about 16 million people could be supported if all land in the area were utilized and present-day agricultural techniques were used. Not all land is suitable for agriculture; perhaps the proportion over all the area is no more than 50 percent, thus lowering our population figure to 8 million, for a reliable estimate. But through more intensive use the area cultivated should have been more productive than now, if the above hypotheses on prehistoric techniques are correct. Poor agricultural years would certainly have lowered the carrying capacity of the land, perhaps by as much as a third. Landa describes the storage of corn against poor seasons, and Herrera seems to describe a community granary at the time of the Conquest; provision for storage could have partially canceled the effects of bad years. Since Conquest times Yucatan has experienced periodic famines due to bad seasons in maize production, coupled with the near absence of grain storage.

An estimate based on somewhat different data may be tried. The population of Yucatan in 1940 was 416,378. Using Shattuck's figures on per-capita consumption, about 90 million kilograms of maize per year are eaten by the human population in Yucatan. To produce this corn, about 12,000 square kilometers of land must be required, nearly one-third of the total area of the state. According to the available information, a third of the area of Yucatan is now planted in henequen. Only a negligible amount of corn (about 2 percent calculated on a 10-year average) is imported. Although published accounts state that only 23 percent of agricultural land in Yucatan is in use for corn, and of the remainder 70 percent is in henequen, a computation based on the above estimates of corn consumption suggests that the true figure is close to 50 percent for maize. Although parts of the area now used for henequen have a rainfall lower than that desirable for corn, it seems likely that if all land in Yucatan were used for corn, an amount double the present consumption might be raised. This would allow a population of 800,000 for Yucatan alone and, since the area of Yucatan is about a sixth of the lowland area, a population of about 5,000,000 is possible as a maximum for the whole area. This density would be about double the average population density of modern

Mexico, which seems a reasonable figure. It should be emphasized that a maximum population for the subsistence crop may never have been reached, and it is likely that evidence given above on the building activities of the Maya does not require us to assume a population of such density.

Bonampak, by Agustín Villagra, Mexico, 1949, illustrates the murals. Morris Steggerda's Maya Indians of Yucatan, Washington, 1941, gives data on Maya agriculture.

IV. THE POST CLASSIC STAGE

The style of life in meso America changed to a marked degree between 900 and 1000 A.D. The Classic stage, characterized by an intricate iconography in its art, a great concentration of community effort on religion, and by the flowering of distinctive, closely integrated and admirably executed regional art styles was superseded. The trends were toward the political expansion of groups centered in central Mexico by means which, at various times and places, probably included militaristic conquest, religious evangelization, economic penetration, and colonization. The geographic extent of these influences is surprising. To the northwest they are recognizable archeologically as far as Guasave, Sinaloa, near the Mexican west coast; to the south they are recognizable linguistically as far as Panama, and archeologically possible as far as Ecuador. There is evidence that the more distant regions were reached by coastal sea traffic in large dugout canoes.

Although the causes which fathered such striking political expansion are mirrored but darkly in the archeological remains of the Valley of Mexico, some hint of its background may be obtained there. After the abandonment of the great ceremonial center at Teotihuacan, which was seemingly destroyed by fire between 600 and 700 A.D., there are no known imposing religious centers active for a period of perhaps 200 years, but there are remains of concentrated settlements with small religious shrines. This evidence suggests the possibility of a violent anticlerical revolution, although native documents describe an invasion. Following this period came the building of the ceremonial center of Tula from which, according to widespread meso American tradition and archeological evidence, the great political expansions began. The Toltecs from Tula are said to have been influenced by more culturally advanced peoples in the vicinity of modern Puebla, and there is archeological evidence of this. The Toltecs also made their own contribution to meso American religious tradition in Quetzal-

coatl, their king and god.   Traces of a feathered serpent,
identified by the Toltecs as Quetzalcoatl, are found in the religious beliefs and art of peoples over an amazingly large part
of the New World.

The peoples of meso America must all have been influenced,
as were the Maya, by the same forces as the Toltecs, even if
Toltec customs were not inflicted forcibly upon them. In the
central Maya area at about 800 A.D., as in several other parts
of meso America, there are archeological evidences of the
breakdown of the closely integrated, religiously centered cultures of the Classic Stage, of an increase in militarism, of the
adoption of human sacrifice, of imported trade goods, and,
in some areas, of the concentration of populations into forti-
fied towns. In fact, in areas as remote as the Mississippi Valley
and in Peru somewhat similar changes in mode of life were
taking place at approximately the same time. The evidence is
still scanty, but it seems likely that ideas rather than governments were at the bottom of these innovations; that the Toltecs
were a symptom rather than a cause. If the ruling priests
among various American peoples were unable to quell a widespread popular ferment, more popular governments may have
succeeded them, and if populations increased under a less rigid
government, military conquest may have started in the Valley
of Mexico as a relief to population pressure.

The impact of these widespread changes on the Maya is well
documented. The central Maya area had suffered a gradual
disintegration of priestly power well before Toltec times, and
it is to this period that social   restlessness, if such there was,
should be ascribed. There is no evidence of violence associated
with the decadence of Classic Maya culture, only a gradual
diminution and final disappearance of Maya ceremonial culture; a political transition in the mild and philosophical Maya
manner seems indicated. The situation in the highland Maya
area is less certain because of scarcity of archeological information on this period there. It has been suggested by some that
the disintegration of priestly government in the central Maya
area may have been due to, or hastened by, land exhaustion
caused in turn by long-continued and intensive agriculture, or
by climatic change. There is evidence against any perceptible
climatic change, but agricultural land exhaustion may well
have played a part.

The culture of northern Yucatan at the close of the Classic
stage appears to have been an outgrowth of a northern focus
which must be considered indigenous in the Puuc-Chenes-Rio

Bec area, and which is archeologically distinguished by finely finished "veneer" style stone masonry, with zones decorated in repeat designs by elaborately carved stones set mosaic-like into a mortar backing. Slateware pottery is found constantly associated with this style of masonry, and Initial Series inscribed stelæ are lacking. The plans of the ceremonial centers of this area are more widely spaced and more informal than those of the central area. Palace type buildings surrounding quadrangular plazas, and larger multistoried palaces, are commoner than are the temples on massive pyramids which predominate on the central Maya Classic sites. A political boundary may have

FIG. 22—BATTLE SCENE AT A MAYA VILLAGE. INNER CHAMBER OF JAGUAR TEMPLE, CHICHEN ITZA. (After a drawing by Adele Breton)

divided the Rio Bec and Peten areas. The archeological picture would seem to be one of a distinct culture and political units to the north, perhaps characterized by a less formal rule than that to the south. The northern late Classic stage culture shows western influence, and the contemporaneous Mexican highland cultures may in turn have been influenced from as far east as Yucatan, although influence going in this direction must be judged as minor on present evidence.

The beginning of the post Classic stage in Yucatan is marked by a strong influx of Toltec influence at Chichen Itza, which would seem to have become the governmental center of Yucatan at this time. The two main sources of evidence there are architectural and ceramic.

The architecture of the Toltec buildings of Chichen Itza stands in strong contrast to the earlier Yucatan late Classic stage architecture of the site. Innovations include vast colonnades which supported Maya type corbel vaults, and large enclosed rooms with beamed, column-supported roofs. The construction of interior open courtyards surrounded by colonnaded galleries, temples of circular plan, the use of a battered basal zone on exterior building walls rather than the Maya vertical wall are further Toltec traits, as is the tendency toward decora-

a   b

FIG. 23—WARRIORS OF THE TOLTEC PERIOD, FROM THE LOWER CHAMBER, JAGUAR TEMPLE, CHICHEN ITZA. *a:* Maya warrior with spear and rectangular shield. *b:* Toltec warrior with spear-thrower and darts, and butterfly breastplate and headdress ornament. (Drawn after Maudslay)

tion by bas-relief carving cut on a flat masonry wall surface rather than the built-up mosaic decoration of the northern Classic Maya.

Architectural decoration at Chichen Itza in the form of sculpture in the round, bas-reliefs and mural paintings (see fig. 22), as well as decorative designs on other than architectural objects, gives a far more complete and sensitive record of Maya-Toltec interaction than does any other archeological line of evidence. The art of the Toltec period is more naturalistic and narrative than that of the northern Maya, abounds in generalized Mexican stylistic traits, and shows many specific identities with that of Tula in the Valley of Mexico. The greatest quantity of such representational material is the several hundred figures of warriors and various functionaries shown singly on the faces of the square columns in colonnades. Many of these figures are clad in elaborate costumes and insignia identical to those on columns at Tula. The same close similarities are observable on figures in processions and in less formal scenes in bas-relief. The Toltecs seem to have introduced the throwing-stick and new types of shields, presumably as superior weapons, and a new type of one-piece battle dress not unlike Churchill's "siren suit." Other figures show costuming close to that on Classic Maya sculptures, and some show costumes with elements traceable to both sources (see fig. 23).

Certain of the bas-reliefs, murals, and repoussé designs on gold discs from the Sacred Cenote at Chichen Itza have a narrational character, and show scenes of warfare in which the Maya are unquestionably on the losing side. Prowling jaguars are shown very similarly in bas-relief at Tula and at Chichen Itza, as are vultures, and certain stylized figures which seem to represent the Mexican rain god Tlaloc (see fig. 24). The murals include depictions of human sacrifice, with the heart removed through the abdomen in the manner used by the Aztecs at conquest times.

Among the architectural-sculptural elements introduced are strange, awkwardly reclining figures called *chacmools*, with bowls carved into their abdomens, thrones in the form of standing jaguars, columns in the form of feathered serpents as door-lintel supports, sculptured figures cut to support flagpoles, human figures sculptured in the round for use in supporting bench-like altars on their heads or arms (Atlanteans), and larger similar figures used as lintel supports.

The list could be lengthened. Some of these traits are duplicated at Tula, others have precursers elsewhere on the Mexican mainland, the origins of still others are uncertain. Some close parallels to bas-relief sculpture in central Veracruz are notable.

Some generalizations can be made as to the kinds of relationships between peoples which could have produced such a composite. The craftsmanship of the sculptures is unquestionably Maya. There is a grace and quality of curve and surface even on those with the closest Tula parallels which is distinctively and unmistakably Maya. The general style of depiction, however, as well as the objects shown, is just as unquestionably

FIG. 24—COMPARISON OF BAS-RELIEF SCULPTURE FROM CHICHEN ITZA, YUCATAN, AND FROM TULA, HIDALGO. *a, b:* A vulture which seems to be eating a human heart. *c, d:* A prowling jaguar. *a, c:* From Chichen Itza. *b, d:* From Tula. (Drawn from photos by T. A. Willard and Jorge Acosta)

that seen at Tula. In the architectural detail the same situation is found. The forms of buildings, columns, figures are Toltec or at least Mexican mainland; the manner of execution is Maya. The superior Maya vault was used, though supported on Toltec style columns and wooden beaming so inadequate that the vaulting must have fallen not long after construction.

The draftsmen and architects must have been Toltec, the craftsmen and laborers unquestionably Maya, and skilled enough so that we may suspect that they were unhappy under their less skilled overlords.

The pottery of this period at Chichen Itza shows an equally strong foreign influence, here predominantly from central Veracruz. There a pottery much superior both technically and artistically both to Tula and to Yucatecan pottery was made and traded to Chichen Itza in quantity. Somewhat surprisingly, much more of this luxury ware reached Chichen Itza than reached Tula, perhaps because of the ease of water transportation, or because of greater economic strength at Chichen Itza, which surpassed Tula both in quantity and quality of architecture. The locally made pottery of Chichen Itza shows copying of the Veracruz Fine Orange wares in form and in design, but a strong adherence to local craft techniques.

The Yucatecan Maya Conquest period stories of these Toltecs show a mixture of attitudes toward them. The Maya revered Quetzalcoatl, who they believed first brought the Mexicans to Yucatan, but deplored various licentious Mexican customs and certain rulers of Mexican descent. This suggests that Toltec religion may have been more easily assimilated by the Yucatecans than was Toltec government, a situation with many parallels in world history. By the time of the Conquest surprisingly few evidences of Mexican customs and language were still observable in Yucatan. This rapid shedding of Mexican influence was likely possible because Mexican innovations were limited to the higher social castes, whose loss of power before the Conquest in Yucatan is well documented.

The earliest metal objects found in the Maya area, save for a few isolated pieces from late Classic sites, come from this period. By far the majority of the metal comes from the Sacred Cenote at Chichen Itza, into which objects were cast as sacrifices. There is no evidence that the copper and gold objects found were ever used as tools. The most beautifully made objects are ornaments which were brought in from Panama and adjacent areas. Metallurgy was known early in Peru, and penetrated but slowly north of there. With little question organized warfare, although previously not completely unknown to the Maya, progressed both in frequency and in technique.

There are indications that the settlement pattern of Yucatan may have been changed by the Toltecs. The Puuc region was heavily occupied at the time of the Toltec conquest, seems to have been nearly abandoned after that time, and has never been settled since. The region has rich soil and plentiful rain-fall, but almost a complete lack of dry season water sources. The water table is too deep to allow Maya style wells, and the inhabitants depended upon excavated cisterns which collected water from paved areas around their mouths. I have calculated that the main plazas of Uxmal alone, if used efficiently as col-lecting basins, could have kept 6000 people in drinking water through the year. Cisterns were seldom dug in the northern Yucatan plain, where cenotes and shallow wells must have sufficed. The Puuc ceremonial sites do not seem to have been lived in, and numerous small ruins, each with a low paved plat-form bearing one or two simple structures and draining into a cistern, dot the areas between the large ruins. These look like the remains of a diffused population pattern of a type similar to that of the Classic stage in the Peten.

There is both documentary and archeological evidence of a shift of the capital city of Yucatan from Chichen Itza to Mayapan part-way through the post Classic stage. The late post Classic occupancy at Mayapan seems to have been of a distinctively different and far more concentrated type than that of the Puuc region. The religious ceremonial precinct lies near the center of a large walled enclosure. The dwelling houses are arranged within the wall, in a manner not unlike that of modern Maya towns. Each has a walled yard around it, and meandering lanes run through the town. No settlement of this type has been reported around the earlier site of Chichen Itza, although remnants of a surrounding wall have recently been reported. There is much evidence of a lingering of pre-Toltec ceramic and architectural techniques at Toltec Chichen Itza, and it is possible that the settling of people close around the temples proceeded slowly and irregularly in Yucatan.

With little question "city-life" in Yucatan must have been introduced through Mexican influence. Teotihuacan is our earliest example of an urban settlement in meso America and, as Eric Thompson has pointed out, the Yucatecan Maya word for town is of Aztec origin. The buildings at Mayapan, like those of modern Yuactecan towns, were loosely spaced. Con-siderable fruit and vegetables are raised within the town, and were at the time of the Conquest. This stands in sharp con-trast to Teotihuacan and other Valley of Mexico towns, where structures were contiguous. Yucatecan urbanism bears a strong rural flavor; the town plans are a bit like those of small towns in the United States.

It is interesting to speculate how and why this striking change in Maya living pattern was introduced. Climatic change and soil exhaustion can probably be ruled out as reasons for the abandonment of the Puuc area. A political cause seems more likely. Perhaps the invading Toltecs compelled the Yucatecans to move into larger, more easily policed and controlled settlements. North Yucatan, with its cenotes perennially full of drinking water, must have appeared more attractive to the Mexicans for large town settlements than did the agriculturally rich but waterless Puuc area. The Classic Maya probably surrounded their isolated houses with produce gardens and fruit trees, and when brought to towns clung to this pattern.

The political history of the post Classic period, as revealed by the Chilam Balams, traditional histories recorded in European script after the Conquest, was notable for bickering and treachery. The events recorded and the prophecies for the future were morbidly pessimistic. In a pattern nearly universal in conquered countries, the foreign rulers seem to have become Yucatecanized and, although Nahua origins seem to have been prized among the rulers, acculturation and intermarriage blurred Mexican-Maya distinctions. The government, when it was established at Mayapan in the thirteenth century, consisted of a confederation of three regional rulers who must have divided their time between Mayapan and their home capitals. This government was broken when one of the rulers brought in Mexican mercenaries from the Aztec garrison at Xicalango about 1450. After this time, rule was divided and times were difficult. This pattern of confederacy, the general style of political history, and archeological evidence of religious influence and of trade in objects from the west, all attest continued Mexican mainland influence. We know, however, that Aztec rule never extended to Yucatan.

The best preserved archeological site of this late period is Tulum, on the east coast of Yucatan (see fig. 25). Most of the buildings there have flat, beamed roofs. Masonry is somewhat haphazard, but notable for massive, smooth stucco facings, many of which bore murals. Plastic decoration of buildings is almost exclusively limited to recessed panels over the doors. The style is striking and distinctive. A fine group of murals of this period has been uncovered farther down the east coast at Santa Rita, British Honduras. The style of drawing and the iconography of these and of the murals are close enough to those of Mitla and to the codices drawn in Oaxaca at this date to make it certain that the religions of the two

FIG. 25—THE CASTILLO AT TULUM, QUINTANA ROO. Tulum, a walled Maya site on the east coast of the Yucatan Peninsula, is the best-preserved of the late post Classic Maya ruins. (Photo by Giles G. Healey)

regions were in close intercommunication. The anthropomorphic incense burners which flooded religious centers all over the Yucatan Peninsula at this time suggest a mass conversion to a religion of Mexican mainland origin. A contemporaneous wave of central Mexican religious influence is documented as far north and west as Guasave, Sinaloa, which is as far in this direction as meso American culture ever reached. To the southeast, the presence of Nahua-speaking colonies as far south as Panama suggests actual colonization which may date from this period or earlier.

The exact nature of this Mixtec-Puebla expansion, as Vaillant has called it, is dubious. Ekholm hypothesizes a migration of peoples to account for his finds at Guasave, Sinaloa, and such a cause, accompanied perhaps by military conquest, and religious conversion seems the easiest explanation for the East Coast and Panamanian evidence. In Yucatan there is evidence of limited immigration at the Toltec period, less evidence later, and no evidence for a foreign government or an imposed language during the later Mayapan period. Mexican highland religion would seem to have been the fire which sparked this tremendous cultural and physical expansion. Its demonstration through both archeological and documentary studies may eventually yield general information on the workings of such movements.

V. THE POST CONQUEST STAGE

The Spanish conquest of Yucatan has little of the romantic interest of the campaigns in Mexico and Peru. The dearth of mineral riches, and for that matter of all spectacular luxury goods in Yucatan, prompted Cortez to bypass the Peninsula after minor skirmishes, and to proceed to Mexico City. Francisco de Montejo and his son, with other Spanish soldiers and gentry, pacified the major centers of the Peninsula in 1544, after many vicissitudes. The country, however, may be considered to have always had a frontier, and discontented Maya have traditionally moved away from authority to the south and east. Even now governmental authority is weak in Quintana Roo; a major uprising of the Indian population, the War of the Castes, began as late as 1847 and lasted into the present century. Quintana Roo has only recently been changed from a territory to a state.

The present population is concentrated in the northern Yucatan peninsula, with a density in the state of Yucatan of about 30 persons per square mile—double the average density of Mexico. In Campeche and Quintana Roo, however, the situation is strikingly different, with densities of only about 6 and 1 persons per square mile respectively. The population of Yucatan since the Spanish conquest has remained at a far more constant figure than that of Mexico as a whole, having increased about 30 percent as compared to an increase of nearly 500 percent for all of Mexico since 1790. The sparse settlement of Quintana Roo and inland Campeche has not changed markedly in a thousand years.

This conservatism in population density through time is linked to an economy which seems to have remained equally conservative. Yucatan agriculture has changed little since the Conquest, and despite the rise of the cattle ranches, henequen, silk production, indigo, logwood, and chicle industries, and a decline of the export of salt, cotton cloth, and beeswax, there has been little economic change in the state. This same conservatism is notable in other fields. For example: whereas in Mexico as a whole about 15 percent of the inhabitants speak a native language, in Yucatan there are 74 percent Maya speakers. This is the highest percentage by far of speakers of a native language in any Mexican state. In Yucatan is also found the highest rate of bilingual inhabitants (Spanish-Maya): 47 percent of the population, as compared to 7 percent for Mexico as a whole. A marked conservatism is also evident in the ceramic industry, where I find that the Toltec conquest caused a greater change than did the Spanish. Some of this conservatism may be due to the non-adoption of glaze in Yucatan. The potters claim that lime in the clay does not permit the use of glaze, but there is further evidence for conservatism in that Yucatecan forming methods, as well as most forms and finishes, date from pre-Conquest times. Architectural construction in both wood and stone also shows abundant evidence of pre-Conquest techniques. Innovations are the minimum ascribable to the use of steel tools, the use of jack vaulting, and changes of architectural style, and are limited, as would be expected, to churches and the houses of the wealthy.

La Farge and Beals have formulated classifications of the post Conquest history of Guatemala and Mexico respectively. Both divide the Spanish colonial period into an earlier stage terminating about 1720, with certain Spanish governmental reforms which lessened the power of Spanish landowners over the Indians. After this stage, the pressure to adopt European ways was slackened as Spanish power decreased. In Yucatan the assignment of Indians as subjects to Spanish hacienda owners, although not legal, was effective in practice until Mexican independence in the 1820's. There is additional evidence of conservatism as well as of relative non-mixing of Spanish and Indian racial stock throughout the Colonial period.

Of the changes wrought by the early Spanish settlement, Catholicism and cattle ranching perhaps penetrated most deeply into Indian life. Certain aspects of Catholic dogma, such as patrons for days and the use of baptismal rites, are not far from ancient Maya observance. The composite nature of Catholicism as practised by meso American Indians is well known and easily recognizable. It is also true that Catholicism has not entirely displaced the Maya religion in relation to the cultivation of land, and that the ancient Maya deities are still invoked to bring wind and rain at their proper seasons. Vestiges of the calendar of sacrifices which ruled the lives of the Maya still persist, as does the custom of making pilgrimages to the old religious centers. The modern mixture of Pagan and Catholic religion is stable and long accepted; the conflict of the 16th century with its *autos de fe* and inquisitorial tactics is dead, with Catholicism the benevolent victor in formal religion.

Cattle ranching remains a thorn to the Maya farmer, whose crop losses and labor in fencing are augmented by the presence of cattle near his corn patch. The principal introduced industries now are henequen raising, cane-sugar farming, and chicle gathering. Of these, chicle gathering is seasonal, fits easily into the framework of Maya life and is pursued only in the uninhabited areas; cane-sugar farming is highly localized to the areas of deep soil and is to some degree mechanized. Henequen raising, which is now a major factor in the economy of Yucatan, began in the last century and was developed by men with financial capital and large land holdings. The Maya labor force lived on the land, and was paid and given perquisites. This system was subject to many abuses. The reforms made in the 1920s and 1930s were radical, consisting of the confiscation of lands and their use under a series of communally run *ejiditarios*. Under President Aleman the laws were modified to allow the gathering and processing of henequen by private capitalists, apparently a more efficient production system than the socialistic one which preceded it. The henequen market is subject to wide fluctuations in price. Wars have produced the most prosperous periods through the cuts they have made in the supply of competitive fiber to the United States. A decline in prices of henequen through the years has been caused by growing competition from other areas against what was originally a Yucatan monopoly, and through a decline in the use of henequen twine for tieing wheat sheaves. At present, Mexican statistics show Yucatan as about 70 percent in henequen and 30 percent in other crops. Although the official percentage figures for henequen are probably too high, there is still not enough crop diversification to provide a stable economy for the state.

Yucatan is singularly isolated from the rest of the world at present. Imports are small and depend primarily upon henequen sales for financing. Henequen is carried out on freighters. Passenger traffic into the country is limited to that by air, which is expensive, a little by sea, where sailings are irregular, and to a negligible amount overland.

It seems likely, from the archeological distribution of artifacts, that during Classic times meso American trade was mainly overland. In Yucatan, for example, the relatively small amount of trade during this period seems to have come from the inland areas. By Toltec times this picture had changed radically; the most striking imports were Panamanian gold and Veracruz pottery, both brought along the coast in the dugout canoes which figure so prominently in the Chichen Itza murals. The complete absence of archeological trade between Yucatan and the Antilles allows a sharp limit to be drawn as to the character of meso American seamanship. The passage between Yucatan and Cuba measures about 125 miles, but is notable for a wicked current. This short but untraversed open water distance contrasts sharply with the remarkable distances traveled by coastal trading vessels.

Yucatan is at present far from the front of human progress —a quiet, backward country. There is certainly no reason to predict that the Maya will again rise to the leadership of civilization in the New World. In the Old World, as well as in the Americas, the first great civilizations developed in warm countries. It was not until the invention of the chimney in twelfth century Europe that the peoples of the temperate zone attained enough comfort and leisure to think abstractly as well as to earn a living. It is only since that time that western European civilization has engulfed the world.

This study of a civilization based on such different standards from ours may lead us to question whether our goals present the only path to human perfection. If the Maya had succeeded the Mexicans as a political power, the Greeks had succeeded the Romans, and the Spanish had conquered the English, the modern world would have been far different! The practical application of the results of intellectual curiosity seems to have been curiously neglected by the Maya who, although living under a simple economy, progressed further in abstract thought than any other New World people. As we learn more of the Maya and of other civilizations, we may be better able to judge the common essential factors which govern human intellectual progress. The Maya erred and fell; failures in the modern world are becoming more expensive at an alarming rate. If study of Maya archeology should eventually shed light on modern problems, the archeologist would follow the atomic physicist out of his ivory tower. But human culture is subject to more complex and variable factors than is physical science. The Maya archeologist still has a long and contemplative road to travel!

Information on Maya archeological sites of the post Classic stage may be found in Earl H. Morris' *The Temple of the Warriors at Chichen Itza, Yucatan*, 2 vols., Washington, 1931, in S. K. Lothrop's *Tulum*, Washington, 1924, and in Lothrop's *Metals from the Cenote of Sacrifice, Chichen Itza, Yucatan*, Cambridge, 1952.